Did you know that men become emotionally available or unavailable for psychologically predictable reasons? The problem that many women face, however, is a lack of knowledge of the conscious and subconscious psychological factors that make men into good or bad bets for committed relationships. Women looking for committed relationships need to understand the specific factors that make men emotionally available and how women can go about finding and getting involved with them. Women should understand how deep-seated psychological influences operate behind the scenes to keep certain types of men immature and emotionally unavailable long after they should have learned how to act their age, and learn whether men who seem to be lost causes can become good bets for committed relationships.

What Makes Men Emotionally Available

**Understanding The Real Reasons
Why Men Do And Don't Want
To Open Up And Get Involved**

ANDREW DOLAN

What Makes Men Emotionally Available
Understanding The Real Reasons Why Men Do And Don't Want To Open Up And Get Involved

ISBN: 1453788956
ISBN-13/EAN: 9781453788950

https://www.Createspace.com/3479973
http://www.Amazon.com/dp/1453788956

Table Of Contents

Chapter One
How Social Roles Shape
Emotional Availability

Emotional Availability And Social Roles

Emotional availability is an adult psychological capacity related to society's definition of what makes a man or a woman an adult. While the details of what constitutes an adult varies from one society to another, one factor does remain constant across different societies. Moving up from being a social adolescent to a social adult means expanding your repertoire of social roles from a single social role for a single social audience, such as that of college student dependent on one's parents, to fulfilling multiple social roles for multiple social audiences, meaning roles such as worker, spouse, father and other roles.

Emotionally unavailable men are typically men who cannot bridge the gap and take on the multiple roles that being a true adult requires. They instead remain frozen in either a single non-adult role, such as that of an emotionlessly monochromatic workaholic, or get sidetracked into non-adult roles, such as gang member, that preclude the development of emotional availability and various other capacities of psychological adults. Men who do not take on multiple social roles are thus incapable of becoming either adults or emotionally available.

A role is whatever you think, say and do to meet the expectations of a social audience of one or more people, and most people act out several social roles in the course of a day. A married man with children who holds down a full-time job while attending college on weekends acts out several social roles for different audiences. Each audience has different behavioral expectations for him, and he must tune out some out-of-sight social audiences when engaged in taking on a social role for his social audience of the moment. As a weekend college student, he fulfills one social role for his professor: the role of student who meets the professor's expectations that he show up for class, hand in assignments on time and prepare for exams. He takes on a different social role with his wife: the role of spouse and companion.

He takes on yet another role with his children: the role of playful father. Finally, he takes on yet another social role with his employer: the role of employee, wherein he complies with his employer's workplace behavior expectations so he can continue to receive paychecks. Each audience has little knowledge of, or interest in, whatever other social roles he might take on for other social audiences. Successfully taking on a social role usually results in him receiving some sort of benefit or reward, such as a paycheck, in return for acting out a given social role for an audience. These rewards for acting out a role are also known as reinforcements, because they reinforce the likelihood of such behavior being repeated because they produce payoffs.

Taking on varied social roles transforms a man into a more socially versatile and psychologically integrated member of a society than a man who focuses his efforts on meeting the behavioral expectations of only one social audience, such as a man who lives with his parents. Men who can meet the expectations of a wide variety of social audiences tend to be successful participants in several parts of their societies, and confident about themselves and their place in society by virtue of the social status others confer on them because they successfully take on varied social roles for other people.

Emotional availability develops as a byproduct of taking on multiple social roles for different social audiences with varied behavioral expectations, allowing men to develop broad-gauged communicative and expressive skills that are useful in both public roles and private relationships. As men get more practice at disclosing limited parts of their true selves to different social groups, they develop a psychological home base from which they can go out and gradually explore greater self-disclosure and emotional expression in one-on-one intimate relationships.

Emotional availability means that a man is available to freely express his emotions with a compatible woman, in part because he has no exclusionary relationships blocking him from forming emotional bonds and engaging in emotional expression. Examples of exclusionary relationships that block emotional availability include a man involved with another woman and a man whose social conditioning with other men has rendered him too immature to engage in adult relationships with women, as happens with men habitually involved as street gang members. Being a street gang member is a social role whose inherent nature requires that a gang member turn his back on taking on other roles such as that of self-supporting adult employed in mainstream society.

Taking on multiple social roles produces multiple forms of psychological satisfaction that provide some relief from the stress produced by taking on any single social role. One example is when a man who is overwhelmed by his job dissipates some of his stress after hours by taking on a more relaxed role with one or more companions. Reducing stress enhances the prospects for emotional availability, because reducing stress makes men feel less threatened about opening up and communicating how they feel. Multiple-role men are a woman's best general bets for emotional availability, because low stress combined with the communicative and expressive competencies acquired as a byproduct of taking on multiple social roles maximizes the chances of a man being emotionally available, though they do not guarantee it in and of themselves. This is a necessary condition for emotional availability, but sufficient in and of itself.

Any single social role brings along with it psychological and pluses and minuses. Paychecks are nice to get, but some aspects of the workplace role you have to act out to get those paychecks can induce stress, and stress reduces emotional availability. The net effect is that, should one role produce a downside on any given day, the other roles you play usually, but not always, produce some countervailing psychological benefits, such as backpatting-style reinforcement by members of the audiences for various role performances. Social approval from the audience for one social role will counteract and dilute the stress produced by the downside of another social role. When water pours in from several fountains into your psychological-emotional bucket, it is not the end of the world when one fountain dries up for a spell.

Income does not determine adulthood or emotional availability. A man might earn a low wage as a manual laborer and yet be reasonably psychologically content with his social status as a gainfully and continuously employed male of the species who has been happily married for ten years, owns a home with his wife, goes fishing regularly, has children learning to become adults themselves and enjoys the comradeship of his co-workers and fellow fishing club members. He fulfills multiple roles with a fair degree of success within the confines of his working-class social environment. By contrast, consider the case of a high-income, unmarried computer programmer who lives and breathes nothing but programming. He has probably suffered a string of unsuccessful relationships due to his unwillingness to leave behind his workplace thoughts and adjust his thinking and behavior to fit into a different frame of reference when attempting to become intimate with women. He is a one-role man, meaning a one-trick pony with a one-track mind. Whatever his financial successes, he is neither psychologically adult nor is he emotionally available. He refuses to tune out his self-imposed workplace social role behavior expectations and fails to tune into what the girlfriend audience expects of him when he is with her. Outside of his job, he does not have much of an adult life. Thinking of himself as a programmer round the clock freezes out his ability to take on other social roles when he is not programming.

Stress increases in proportion to the degree to which one social role defines the individual. Stress reduces the mental wiggle room you feel you have for opening up in relationships and enjoying yourself. Acting out several different roles makes it easier to take on an emotionally available role with others, because you have other psychological inputs feeding a variety of feelings into your mind as well as more social-skills ambidexterity for use in dealing with varied kinds of people and social situations. Emotionally complete adults must be able to tune into varied social audiences if they are to be considered fully functioning adults. Single-role men who live and breathe only one role, such as that of tough-guy-for-all-occasions, have more stressful lives than multiple-role men. They are totally dependent on one role for all of their social satisfaction. Should your one source of the psychological water of satisfaction with life dry up, your psyche will be left distressingly high and dry. Your reservoir of emotional availability dries up as the heat pressure of role stress rises and you become a less relaxed, less emotionally available companion.

Career military men from impoverished backgrounds whose entire self-definition depends on their military rank may be unable to drop their organizational workplace roles when at home and are away from the public audience for the workplace role they take on in the military. Grown men who act like "little boys" are another case in point. Emotionally immature "little-boy" behavior is a juvenile role men learn early in life by tuning into the expectations of male peer groups. This social role offers nothing to women, but men are subjected to ongoing social pressure from male peer group members to continually act like emotionally superficial little boys and block off opportunities to learn how relate to women in more adult ways as a condition for continued social acceptance among their peers, as happens in street gangs and fraternities.

When men get too much practice at scaling themselves down to what their public social roles require of them, their scaled-back emotions become the psychological template for both their public and private lives. They get too much psychological reinforcement in their job roles to want to consider taking on different roles in other social contexts. Social roles such as workaholic roles, and peer-group roles such as street gang member, often program an individual's emotions in ways that are contextually appropriate for one social role, but wholly inappropriate for private-life roles.

One-role men are unable to tune out the behavioral expectations of audiences irrelevant to other social contexts. One social role becomes the template for the other parts of a man's life, such as a street gang member who continually acts out his tough-guy role in every other part of life. No matter how well a man or woman plays any single social role, one-role people remain incompletely adult. Being an adult requires taking on and living more than one social role. Living to fulfill only one role all day and night flattens and pains the personality just as standing on a concrete floor all day flattens and pains the feet.

As you get used to disclosing different aspects of your true self to a number of social audiences, it becomes less of a giant step to disclose a larger portion of your true self to one particular intimate companion. The stress-dilution effect of taking on multiple roles reduces the one-role stress that tends to block the expression, and development of emotional availability. Having experience in partial self-disclosure in the course of fulfilling varied social roles adds to your ability to more fully disclose your true self to others. Having opportunities to learn how to relax and open up to members of the other sex is another factor that contributes to building foundation for emotional availability. This applies equally to both men and women. Men learn about how women think and how to deal with them in the process of taking on, and learning, social roles wherein women are the audience for such roles.

Single And Multiple Roles

Human beings are genetically and psychologically hardwired to fulfill multiple social roles for diverse social audiences. This capacity for taking on roles was built into the human species by millions of years of evolution in a social environment of small tribes and clans where each person had to fulfill several different specialized social roles in the course of day. Hunter-gatherers had to be mates, parents, animal hunters or plant gatherers, members of the tribe or clan and participants in tribal celebrations. Most of us wear several social hats in the course of a single day, quite unlike ants, meaning queen bees and drones, who are psychologically hardwired by their species' genetic code with the capacity to perform one, and only one, single inflexible social role.

The environment we evolved in had no niches for one-note role players who wanted to do only one thing all day long. You could not get by being just a hunter, just taking care of children or just by being the tribal storyteller. Everyone had to do several different things at different times of day to survive. The idea of being just a worker, just a housewife or just a street gang member is a very recent, and unnatural, social innovation forced onto brains specifically evolved and genetically hardwired by evolution to take on multiple roles during the course of a day. Regardless of how much our societies change, we still walk around with brains evolved for specific functions in a very different sort of ancestral world.

Only by taking on multiple social roles can the individual get through the day and acquire the social-psychological adaptability and breadth of experience that results in a broad-based set of social and emotional expression competencies and the sense of security that is a prerequisite for being emotionally available. As men become more experienced dealing with varied types of people, they learn to fine-tune their thoughts and behavior to meet the needs of varied social audiences. They come to understand women and slowly develop the skills necessary for expressing themselves with women in an adult manner. Being an emotionally well-rounded individual thus requires previous exploratory experience at acting out a well-rounded repertoire of social roles for diverse social audiences. You gradually learn how to make emotional contact with people as a byproduct of interacting with them, developing inferred understandings of the other sex and fine-tuning your behavior accordingly.

One-role men are bad bets for relationships. Their self-definition derives from taking on one social role, such military drill instructor, workaholic or street gang member. The greater the degree to which some single social role shapes their lives and minds, the less emotionally available they are. Emotional availability requires varied social competencies and the ability to continually adjust one's speech, behavior and thoughts to dealing with different kinds of people. One-role men can't express emotions because their one-role lives preclude them from developing such in the first place. They get little practice at developing different sorts of communicative and expressive skills for different types of people in their one role, and get even less practice at emotional self-disclosure. One-role men practice disclosing only very limited parts of themselves to others. They are worried that others will put them down were they to find out what they lack by way of adult emotions, social competencies and general adaptation to the larger society.

One common form of this one-role syndrome is being a workaholic, meaning that you define yourself in terms of your job and applying whatever gives you satisfaction and social status on that job to every other area of life, including relationships. Job roles are acted out for public, not private, social audiences. You wind up with a one-dimensional social identity and scale down your emotions to whatever level of emotional expression is consistent with applying your job's rigidly unspontaneous standards for self-revelation and emotional expression to your emotional life. Emotional availability is scaled down to whatever is allowed in, expressed in terms of, the job role. Living to fulfill only a job role necessarily scales down emotional availability to whatever third party public audiences for your job role expect and tolerate. It precludes what the two people most directly concerned want, or should want, were they not tied in mental knots of inhibition by trying to weave the threads of an irrelevant public social role into an interpersonal relationship.

The more you try to meld together your public and private roles, the more sure-fire your guarantee of experiencing a social disaster. While taking on multiple roles does not guarantee emotional completeness, it does at least set a precedent by allowing varied opportunities for limited self-disclosure and self-expression in different roles.

A young man who works in a restaurant develops certain social skills in dealing with the public, and other social competencies in socializing with women on the job and after work. He gradually becomes emotionally socialized by interacting with women, coming to understand them and adjusting his behavior when with them.

Add to this the social skills he acquires in other social roles, such as hospital volunteer and after-school tutor, and you have a very different sort of young man than the young man who simply goes to work or school each morning and goes home to his parents at the end of the day. A man who avoids women on the job and goes home to his parents after work every night to watch television stunts his emotional socialization until such time as he starts interacting with women. The role he takes on with his parents imparts nothing to him that he can use to relate to single women.

Emotional Availability Requires Multiple Roles

Emotional availability requires being a social adult, and you are not an adult unless and until you take on multiple social roles. Men who fail to take on multiple social roles for multiple social audiences are incomplete adults who develop, at best, adolescent capacities for emotional expression and availability. Single-role men are strangers to an entire universe of adult concerns, meaning interaction, communication and emotional expression, as any woman who has been involved with an entrepreneur who lives and breathes nothing but his business, or a software programmer who lives in a self-centered electronic world of his own, can testify. What is more, such men do not change as they get older. Until they move beyond their one-role lives, take on different roles, start to understand others and get used to meeting the expectations of different types of people, they might age chronologically, but their minds remain mired in an adolescent-mentality closed loop.

One-role men often become resentful and envious of emotionally available multiple-role men they see having enjoyable, well-rounded lives. One-role men resent other men having a higher perceived quality of life, meaning appearing to enjoy life more than they do. Greater emotional availability allows those other men access to a wide range of more fully adult relationships and well-rounded vocational and community lives that one-role men can not access due to their limited social and emotional competencies. One-role men want what they see, but are unwilling to change and take on additional social roles to equip themselves to enter more fully adult relationships by virtue of having personalities better adjusted for interactions with other emotional adults.

One-role men resent feeling that they are missing out on life, but fail to realize that real adults have nothing to gain from associating with them. Emotional adults can usually spot emotional adolescents a mile away, and want nothing to do with them. Real adults do not seek out non-adults for mature relationships, and non-adults miss out on the pleasures that go with being a true adult by virtue of continuing their adolescent persistence in locking themselves into single roles with no latitude for growth, change and maturation. Aging emotional adolescents get left behind to mix with other aging emotional adolescents who offer each other nothing beyond egocentricity, stilted social skills and temper tantrums. One-role men are one-trick ponies with too much inertial experience at staying emotionally adolescent to learn any new tricks, and associating with others who are also bogged down at that stage of development operates to freeze them at that stage of development.

How Roles Program Your Personality

Human beings are social animals with brains specifically adapted to interact with other human beings in specialized ways that enhance our mutual prospects for survival. Many forms of social interaction derive from our language abilities, and our brains have neuronal arrangements specifically evolved for language. We interact with each other through social roles mediated by language, and take on different roles for different types of people in differing social situations to obtain different sorts of beneficial outcomes or results from our interactions. A hammer serves the function of hitting and driving in a nail, a saw serves the function of cutting wood, and different roles serve similarly divergent functions in varied social settings filled with people with differing behavioral expectations. One role does not suit all social audiences and social occasions any more than you can use a hammer to saw wood or use a saw to hit nails. Roles are customized social adaptation tools developed to suit specific types of social situations and audiences. You can not act the same way with every social audience.

Men can strangle some of their social capacities in the process of fitting themselves into roles where certain capacities may be a detriment to filling that role. Even if certain capacities are considered irrelevant to playing a role, social pressures from those already filling that role – a peer group - can force a man to run his personality through a cookie cutter role-fitting process that trims everyone filling the role down to the same personality configuration. Growing into a role means the role becomes an integral part of your core personality, the part of you that decides which social roles to take on or not take on as well as the relative importance of other roles in your life.

A man might decide to repress his intellectual capacities to better fit into a workplace peer group of manual laborers who put down "book learning." A street gang member might repress his capacity for emotional availability because his street gang role models apply continual social pressures to prevent him from taking on intimate and adult roles with women. Street gang members think that the one role they pressure a member to live up to – street gang member - is the only social role of any kind he should take on. The individual must knuckle under and adapt his personality to conforming to group expectations, not his own needs. Even less should he seek to adapt himself to the private audience of a woman's expectations. Any male peer group that pressures men to extend some single social role to all parts of their lives almost always discourages men from becoming emotionally available. One-role men drown out their potential to take on multiple social roles in the psychological waste products of their single-role lives. The peer group sees loyalty as a zero-sum game: whatever dedication a woman "gets" from a man, they think is "stolen" from a street gang, fraternity, informal drinking club or other male peer group. One social role thus becomes the template for every other part of life, because loyalty to the group comes before everything else, including individual priorities.

How Roles Expand To Fill The Mind

Taking on only one social role means the stresses of that single role will not be counteracted by pleasurable feelings or forms of satisfaction derived from taking on other roles. It is like trying to walk on one leg instead of two. It can be done, but the stress will increase over time, and the leg muscles will increasingly deform over time due to the contortions you put it through. Should you live and breathe your job as the focus of your self-definition, this will eventually taint your emotional availability. You have nothing to "make up" for the resultant stress when one role falls apart, or stops paying off with social status and psychological benefits.

A multiple-role man who loses his job has counterbalancing psychological payoffs from other roles: family man, fishing club member, and so on, to round out his psyche when he loses his job. A one-role man who lives to work might crumble psychologically should he lose his job and with it, the single social role that is the fountain of his self-esteem. An athlete who defines himself solely in terms of his athletic performance, and then crumbles psychologically after becoming injured, is a prime example. A one-role man's mind has a lot of empty space where other roles should be, and the share of mind his single role occupies expands, like hot air, to fill every unoccupied inch of role space in the mind.

A man can take on a social role without it filling up every part of his mind and warping his personality. What matters is not so much how much of the day a role occupies but rather how much of the mind that role occupies. The greater the degree to which he lives and breathes only one social role, the greater the share of mind that one role occupies. A man might psychologically distance himself from a role, as with a role he does not allow to take up a major share of mind, because he cares little about it. An example is a job a man does not care for but which he must work at to keep eating and paying the rent. He might take on a seemingly comprehensive role, such as that of husband, yet taking on the role might have little effect on his inner mental life, as happens in the case of shotgun marriage. His mind is elsewhere.

A man can take on a role but remain psychologically untouched by it because he chooses to not integrate it into the warp and woof of his life. Such a man is "among them but not of them." The share of mind these involuntary, emotionally distant and unwelcome roles occupy remains at the absolute minimum that circumstance will allow. He has no gusto in his heart for these roles. Jobs, roles and marriages and circumstances can be the result of sheer happenstance, pressing circumstances or financial exigencies. A man might thus seem to be taking on multiple roles, but only on the most emotionally distant and superficial level. He does not take these emotionally distant roles into his heart. They mean no more to him than the many possible sets of clothing he takes on and off as circumstances - or roles - require.

More About Emotional Availability

Emotional availability is a learned capacity for spontaneous, self-disclosing, emotionally expressive, two-way communication in a voluntary one-on-one relationship between compatible individuals unhindered by other commitments. It is a form of two-way communication that expresses whatever meets the individual's self-defined needs for intimacy and emotional expression.

Emotionally available men open up emotionally and take on intimate roles only with women they deem individually compatible. They tune out social pressures to commit to women whom they judge to be incompatible with their individual needs and priorities. This means that even if other people tell him that "she's right for you," he does not care what they say unless he has come to the same conclusion entirely on his own. Male commitment is thus individual-specific. Each man has his own definition of compatibility. By contrast, men take on emotionally distant, noncommittal social roles ("just friends") with incompatible women they consider unsuitable for long-term relationships.

Emotional availability requires a low level of stress in a man's life such to help him feel relaxed about "opening up." Relatively unstressed men don't see emotional expression and self-disclosure as things that will tip their stress-loaded minds over the edge and into depression should they be rejected or put down. Emotional availability does require a core adult personality of autonomous individuality developed as a thing apart from the social roles an individual takes on for other purposes. Social roles generally restrict emotional expression as an incidental byproduct of filling such public roles, while individualism enhances the spontaneous expression of genuine unstructured communicative intimacy in the context of one-on-one audiences.

Expressing individuality enhances a man's search for compatible companions he deems worthy of expressing his emotional availability. Individualism encourages the expression of a man's true feelings and ideas. A two-way free flow of information is necessary to continue performing an intimate role for an audience of the other sex. Without a self-disclosing free flow of information about your inner self, you become emotionally unavailable to the other person, because you provide them with no additional information about yourself to which they can react. If they don't know anything about you, they won't open up to you. Emotional availability requires making information about your personality, life history, emotional reactions and personal preferences available to the other person.

Each new person you meet is essentially a new country where you must learn and practice their particular emotional language and customs if you want to benefit from contact with them, or else face the prospect of being permanently marginalized in that individual's private society. If you won't communicate with them, you won't benefit from contact with them. The more you communicate, the greater your chances of benefiting from contact with them. Moving beyond superficial social contact towards intimate communication opens up a world of possibilities beyond what you get from taking on public social roles with them. It requires gradually learning the individualized language of intimate communication with that one other person by slowly growing to understand that other person and tailoring your contacts with that person based on the understandings you infer about them. You can use what you about others as a starting point for interaction, but the degree to which you fail to customize your interactions with a significant other to their personal needs and preferences is the degree to which the relationship is bound to fail. Nobody likes to be treated as a generic member of the other sex, and doing so keeps the gates of intimacy bolted.

Few things are more socially grotesque than a one-role social illiterate taking on a generic workplace role in a private relationship. Such ritualized roles are a threadbare substitute for individualized, spontaneous emotions. Autonomy from one's public social roles encourages, but does not guarantee, emotional availability. Neurotic dependence on non-individualistic public social roles eliminates emotional availability, because acting out a public role leaves a large measure of what goes on in a man's head all day blocked off, repressed and unexpressed.

A man who locks himself into performing roles for third parties is not emotionally available, because he has accepted the basic premises that the behavioral expectations of public audiences, usually meaning male peers, are more important than what he wants for himself and his intimate companion's needs. A man can express his emotions to a woman only when he feels free to experience those emotions in the first place, and men locked into the emotional deepfreeze of public social roles are beyond hope. They just don't get it that they must tune out irrelevant, out-of-sight social audiences and tune into the audience of the here-and-now.

Emotional availability is thus a truthful, spontaneous, individualistic, informal self-revelatory role that arises as a byproduct of developing social competencies such as self-disclosure by taking on multiple roles for varied social audiences. Emotional availability might even be hardwired into our brains by evolution to emerge only when multiple roles have been taken on in the first place. Women sense that emotionally available men are promising potential mates because taking on multiple social roles usually correlates with the relaxation of self associated with the societal definition of social status. Men with social status have something to offer women, even if they are not particularly emotionally available. By contrast, a socially limited one-role man who lives and breathes nothing but his job offers women fewer social adaptation and intimacy skills, because he does not have a wealth of varied social experiences to draw on in his dealings with people in public or private capacities. He lacks both social skills and social status. One-role men are obsessed with getting others to focus on what they do have as a means of blotting out from view what they don't have, meaning adult social skills and emotional competencies. They may be starved for affection, but emotional availability is a two-way street. Emotional starvation does not equal emotional availability. You have to have something to offer others beyond evidence of your starvation.

Romance And Emotional Availability

Romance is not the same as emotional availability. Romance is a shared state of mind, a mutual attraction we all know can easily be unrequited and quite one-sided. Romance results in a positive and euphoric state of mind due to our delight at the prospect of intimacy. By contrast, emotional availability is form of ongoing two-way communication about needs, feelings, interests and intentions. You are born with the capacity for romantic attraction, while you gradually learn to become emotionally available. Romance might develop as a byproduct of a pre-existing form of intimately emotional communication wherein people disclose their authentic feelings to each other. Romance might thus come first and lead to emotional availability, or two people might be emotionally available before meeting each and romance might eventually bloom as they reveal themselves to, and express themselves with, each other.

Romance is an inborn capacity for attraction to another person. Every normal adult with a normal adult brain has a capacity for romantic attraction and communication, though not everyone chooses to acknowledge (to themselves or others) either their capacity or the person who engenders their romance, as anyone who listens to adolescent conversations knows. Romance is an instinctual capacity of both adults and nonadults, an inborn capacity that comes with being human. Even young school boys and school girls can have unrequited romantic feelings and crushes for other students or their teachers.

Emotional availability is not inborn. Like athletic ability, everybody has some capacity for it, but not everybody develops it to the same extent. It is learned behavior. It develops through social interaction, and will not develop in social isolation. It requires learning about what you like in others and how others react to you through actual social interaction. You slowly learn what others are like, you learn how to express your feelings with them as you learn about them and you learn to pick and chose compatible companions. Men become emotionally available by interacting with women, learning about them and gradually learning to fine-tune their thoughts and behavior to meet the expectations and needs of women. A man gradually learns to disclose his true self to a woman in an intimate context by edging into emotional expression with a woman. He does not simply project his own needs, state of mind and theories onto women. Men who fail to move beyond superficial interactions with women never develop the expressive skills, understandings and experiences necessary for emotional availability.

A man can thus be romantic without understanding what women are really like, what their needs are and how to meet them, their mutual compatibility, how to express his emotions and how best to adjust his behavior to becoming intimate with one particular woman. Romance might eventually develop in a relationship as a result of emotional availability, even should real romance not be present right from the start, but it is important to remember that romance and emotional availability are really two separate and distinct things.

A man can be romantic, or appear to be, without being emotionally available. A self-centered workaholic who lives and breathes one social role stifles his potential to become emotionally available because he neither wants to learn about himself and his emotions or how to understand the inner worlds of other people. He might enjoy romantic feelings without having any interest whatsoever in a woman's inner feelings, personality, intimate needs, emotional availability and what she looks for in a man. All he cares about is his own feelings. His notion of romance is a one-sided thing, though it is quite possible for an emotionally unavailable man to get into a superficial romantic relationship with a romantic, but otherwise emotionally unavailable, woman. Men do not have monopoly on emotional unavailability. This is a superficial relationship where two people never get to know much about each other's needs, and emotional availability requires ongoing communication about what each party needs, prefers and enjoys. Many people never get beyond the superficial because they have no idea what lies beyond it or how to go about getting there. The key is for a man to adapt and fine-tune his speech, thoughts and behavior in different ways to both social groups and particular intimate companions, and keep his thoughts about each in two different mental compartments. Some things are best reserved for public audiences, and some are best reserved for private social audiences.

Why Men Commit

Male commitment is individual-specific. Men commit only to women with qualities that match their preexisting, purely-individualistic personal definitions of suitability and role expectations for intimate companions. Individual men commit to individual women who appear to meet their personal expectations for intimate role behavior, and each man has his own definition of how a given woman should fill out the details of an intimate role. Women must appear to match an individual man's expectations, not what men in general expect of women in general.

A given man will become emotionally available only with a woman who fits the image of compatibility he carries around in his head, no different than a casting director seeking a woman who matches up with his mental image of the lead actress he seeks. Men will take on emotionally available roles only with women who appear to be taking on roles they equate with their individual definitions of compatibility.

Men commit to individual women with very particular personal qualities that meet their idiosyncratic, self-determined needs. The more emotionally available the man, the more individualized and highly personalized his interests in women, and the less his susceptibility to external social pressures to commit to women who are incompatible with their individual needs and priorities. Male role expectations for intimate roles with compatible women preclude catering to the role expectations of third-party audiences external to a one-on-one relationship. Tuning into a here-and-now intimate audience requires tuning out the expectations of irrelevant third parties elsewhere. Emotionally available men do not care what those outside the relationship think, expect or pressure them to do in private relationships.

Men do not commit to women who fail to meet their idiosyncratic expectations for female desirability. Emotionally available men take on noncommittal, emotionally distant social roles ("just friends") with women they deem unsuitable for long-term relationships by virtue of insufficient individual incompatibility. Noncommittal men take disinterested roles with incompatible women to discourage unwelcome attempts at intimacy. The less they reveal of themselves, the less chance they give incompatible women to press the issue.

Identification With Others

The ability to identify with others is an inborn human social group instinct. Identification is a psychological process related to the ability to understand and take on different roles. It is the capacity to mentally put yourself in another person's place and see things as they do. When you identify with another person, you see life from their viewpoint, which often means seeing life from the viewpoint of the role, or roles, they take on. Some people choose to develop the capacity to identify with others, and some do not.

Back when the birth of quintuplets with an uncommon event, it was common for total strangers to send money to the parents of the quintuplets. The strangers identified with, and empathized with, the financial straits they knew such parents faced. Anyone with children knew that taking care of even one child requires enormous amounts of energy, time and money, and knew that quintuplets could easily add up to a lot more than any two parents could handle without help. Parents knew that having quintuplets just as easily could have happened to them, and identified with the beleaguered parents' situation.

Some people choose to develop their capacity to identify with others, some do not. As men take on multiple social roles, they generally, but not always, become more likely to identify with others. Taking on roles involves inferring what other think of you and expect of you, meaning you see yourself as they do from their position in your social audience. Some men blindly mimic what they see others doing in taking on certain roles, and never learn how to identify with others and understand what goes on in their heads. If you don't understand, or want to understand, others, you can't identify with them, you can't put yourself in their shoes and you will have a tough time figuring out what others expect of you and how they react to you.

Men who can't identify with women treat them badly in part because they are unable to see their own treatment of women from the point of view of the woman. They fail to adjust how they treat a particular woman on the basis of feedback from her and understanding how things feel from her end of the relationship. No matter how much feedback some men get from women, they simply refuse to identify with a woman and fine-tune their speech, thoughts and behavior. Such men treat women as inanimate objects that happen to talk but are otherwise unworthy of any special effort on their part to figure out.

Identification is a human group instinct that helps bring people together. We tend to identify with others when we think we have some sort of characteristic in common, such as sharing a common viewpoint, belief or background, such as nationality, religion, social class, political beliefs and the like. The opposite is also true: the failure to perceive some sort of common ground gives some people an excuse to not identify with certain individuals or groups of people. They think of those others as being wholly different sorts of beings in some alien category apart from themselves. They therefore don't even try to tune into seeing things as those others do.

This anti-identification, exclusionary behavior ties into another social instinct: territoriality. Territoriality means that anyone outside your self-defined group and its physical or social territory is outside the group's territorial boundaries, the psychological group territory boundaries that allow you to identify and empathize with those others. The stronger the strength of the bond among members of your social group's psychological territory, the more the strength of that bond excludes outsiders, however defined, from sharing that bond and being eligible for identification. Should men not identify with someone, they are far less likely to care about them, their welfare and how they treat or exploit them. Men will not be emotionally available with women should they choose to not identify with the needs of those women. Such men do not fine-tune their speech, thoughts and behavior to reflect an adjustment to the needs of women because they have no insight in the first place into how women they think and see the world. For example, a man who refuses to adjust when and how he touches a woman based on her verbal and nonverbal reactions to him both fails to identify with her and her viewpoint on how he treats her in the relationships. He fails to meet her tactile needs. He is unable to effectively communicate with her due to his lack of understanding of her, and his lack of understanding is rooted in his inability to see things from her point of view. Some men are incapable of understanding things as basic as the female body requiring different paces and modes of sexual stimulation than the male body.

One common mental block against male emotional availability is the bond men form with peer groups of other men. The more ingrained such male peer group roles become, the more they tend to exclude women from eligibility for emotional bonding. They define outsiders, including women, as aliens with whom they can neither identify nor form a close relationship. They will go through the motions and give lip service to things they know women regard, but it goes no further than that. The bond shared by male peer group members focuses and limits their emotional energies and capacities for loyalty, identification and empathy into ways that exclude identifying with women. Such men are not emotionally available.

The stronger the bond between men in some male peer group, the more likely they are to be unable to shift their mental and social gears when with women. Their male peer group bond extends the emotional-claim territory of their semi-tribalistic group loyalty to include limitations on forming emotional bonds with women. Groups such as fraternities, street gangs and drinking clubs program members to identify solely with group members, relegating all outsiders, women included, to the realm of ineligibility for identification by virtue of being "outside" the group's membership-only territory. Women thus become outsiders ripe for exploitation by men unable or unwilling to identify with women.

Chapter Two
One-Trick Ponies With
One-Track Minds

Primary Roles And Satellite Roles

Imagine a large planet such as Jupiter, massive in size and exerting enormous gravitational pull. This massive celestial body has a number of small satellites, each a small fraction of the size of the parent body around which they spin. Satellites are, by definition, secondary to the primary celestial body about which they orbit in paths predetermined by the gravitational influence of the parent body. No matter what happens, a satellite of minor mass is just not going to go about moving beyond the parent body's gravitational influence. It is destined to remain forever a satellite whose path is determined by its peripheral relationship to the parent body. Unless some even more massive celestial body passes nearby and pulls the satellites out of their designated circuits and into a new sphere of influence, they will simply circle about the parent body forever, never knowing anything beyond what they already are.

Many men think their lives are meaningful only in terms of fulfilling one social role as central to their self-definition. One-role men are thus socially programmed by the expectations of others around them. They may also fulfill secondary social roles for other social audiences, but derive gratification only from fulfilling the primary role, not the satellite roles. Consciously or unconsciously, they distance themselves from accepting other roles as psychologically fulfilling. They arbitrarily assign value only to the reinforcement received from fulfilling their primary role. Should you decide only one role has value, you proceed to tune out alternative forms of psychological gratification derived from taking on other social roles. You also refuse to even consider taking on other roles you think might dilute the reinforcement and gratification received from your primary social role. Taking on roles becomes a zero-sum game: the gains from one role are seen as a loss with respect to the primary role. A street gang member's status with his gang is diluted if he takes on a steady job and develops a work ethic, for example. He is one-trick pony with a one-track mind. All of his eggs are in one psychological basket.

Whatever the man sees as his primary or central role in life, be it a self-determined or externally-determined role, the details of filling out and living that role in turn determine the impact roles taken on for other social audiences have on his life. If a man sees himself as an unemotional, coldly calculating, manipulative tough guy, the other parts of his life fall into place as dependent on, and strictly optional, in relationship to his primary social role. Being nice to women takes a back seat to what fraternity brothers or drinking partners think if a man accords primary psychological significance to what his male peer group think of him.

The proof of the pudding is how a man treats women when his male peer group colleagues are around. Regardless of whatever claims to the contrary a man might make, a man whose self-induced primary social role is his relationship to a male peer group will accord the highest regard to that peer group's opinions of his behavior, and not the woman's opinion. He has too much cumulative practice at deferring to male peer opinions and expectations. He will treat women in certain emotionally distant ways because he values male peer opinions of him above both her opinions and even his own opinion of himself and his needs. Having chosen his relationship to a male peer group as his primary social role, his other social roles become mere satellite roles, destined to forever orbit around his primary role, influenced by the psychological gravity of the primary role, but unable to influence the primary source of psychological gravitation themselves. The psychological planetary giant about which his secondary roles orbit is simply a giant mass of psychological dead weight forever destined to remain emotionally inert.

The level of emotional availability and adult development that accompany the primary role he chooses will determine the limits within which his satellite roles will remain circumscribed. Roles create inhibitions that scale down emotional expression to whatever suits the expectations of the audience for that public social role. Whatever limits on emotional availability an emotionally distant tough-guy role allows becomes the limits on emotional availability for whatever other roles a man takes on with women as well. These men are locked into whatever level of emotional availability their peer group – not the individual - deems acceptable as a form of social control over him. Peer groups dislike women exerting any significant level of influence over a man, because the juvenile, emotional zero-sum game standards of the peer group dictate that involvement with a woman reduces the group's control over the individual group member, and control over the individual is the name of the peer-group game.

Whatever attraction and reinforcement a woman exerts over a man is seen by the peer group as competition for control over his mind and time. Whatever she controls is seen as coming at the expense of the peer group. They accord the woman a minor role, or at least demands that the man accord secondary deferential status to women. The peer group's psychological gravitation thus determines the limits of the psychological influence of a woman over a male group member. When the peer group propagandizes that women are to have no real influence over group members, including that attitude as part of the social role the man plays for the male peer group audience also sets emotional limits and constraints on the other roles he half-heartedly plays for other social audiences. The primary social role a man chooses will often carve in stone the level of emotional availability that a man allows himself in other roles.

Men typically spend more time with their peer group colleagues than with members of the other sex, and those peers groups drum their attitudes into men's heads day after day. Should a woman beg a man to change, the man remains subject to ongoing, day-by-day social pressures, conscious and subconscious, from his peer group to conform, to say nothing of the years of prior conditioning he has behind him. An hour-long plea from a woman for change has the comparative psychological weight of a flea compared to the elephant tonnage of cumulative peer-group conditioning at the other end of the scale that he has been accumulating for years, meaning thousands of hours of cumulative peer-group socialization over the course of many years.

The emotionally available man's mind works differently. The roles he takes on either act to expand his emotional availability or have no effect on his emotional availability. His social programming and core personality relegate his other social roles to suitably peripheral orbits around his center of psychological gravity. His primary self-determined social role is to take on only those roles that suit his personal emotional needs and desires for self-expression. Even when forced to take on a role contrary to his core personality, he distances himself emotionally from that role to the degree that circumstances allow, as with a man drafted into the military. When a man's primary, core-personality characteristics are individualism and self-expression, the roles he takes on get arranged around what is already in place in his mind.

One-Trick Ponies With One-Role Lives

We have all met chronological adults who fail to mature emotionally and socially. Some are old and some are young. What they have in common is that some single social role defines nearly every aspect of their lives, regardless of the inappropriateness of that role and role behavior for other areas of life. A street-punk tough guy who acts tough and disinterested on all social occasions is one example. The primary social role such an individual plays is the tough-guy role, and he probably derives most of his self-esteem from playing that role. When he tries playing another role, he gets less respect (probably deservedly so) because he carries over ill-matched attitudes from his tough-guy role to other parts of life. Thus, whatever respect and positive feedback he gets from playing his tough-guy role reinforces the likelihood that he will always take on the tough-guy role on all social occasions. He probably gets no positive feedback in any other area of his life because he is unable to offer other social audiences anything that they appreciate. The tough-guy role is the only part of his life where he feels important so he practices it on all occasions.

Should he have little education, low intelligence or limited social skills, he may unconsciously push himself into this role, and refuse to learn to take on other roles with less immediate payoffs and less perceived social status. In the minds of such men, fear on the part of others in reaction to his dominating behavior is considered positive feedback that makes such behavior more likely to recur. Even education may be shrugged off as not worth the bother. It can't compare with the instant payoff he sees on the faces of others when he takes on his tough guy role. Some young women like tough guys, and should this happen early enough in life, the tough guy role becomes linked in his mind with positive reinforcement in the form of female companionship.

Such men are unlikely to bother to learn to take on other roles. Young tough guys grow older to become socially inept, inarticulate, poorly educated older tough guys who fit in only at the low end of the social scale and the job market, where their sole source of limited social status is likely to be their tough-guy role. Their opportunities to take on other roles fade because the tough guy role gets trotted out on all occasions. A dominating, tough guy manner will probably be the way they always approach relationships, because they associate domination with positive feedback ever since their early years. Unless they see fast and easy social payoffs from taking on other roles, they will probably never bother to even check them out.

Roles Expand To Fill In The Mind's Blank Spots

The greater the extent to which one role defines your daily activities, the greater the extent to which that role expands to fill in the blank spots in your mind. This means that you not only take on behavioral characteristics associated with acting out that role, but also things as nitty-gritty as political and social opinions consistent with that role. Few people expect bankers or accountants to be political and social firebrand liberals, for example. Many people work at living up to their role expectations, in the sense of changing and adjusting their thoughts and behavior to suit what others expect of them in that role.

Multiple roles fill out in an individual's mind, providing several types of psychological satisfaction to counterbalance the stress and dissatisfaction one role might be providing. For example, you might have a bad day on the job, but dissipate your job-related tensions in after-hours socializing in a bar with your co-workers or at home with a significant other. When you take on several roles for different social audiences during the course of day, the total pluses and minuses of the stresses and benefits of all the roles you take on tend to even out in your mind and keep you on an even keel. One-role workaholics who live and breathe their jobs do not have this option. Their single roles provide only a limited amount of positive feelings. The only payoff from a high-status, high-stress job such as commodities trader might be the financial compensation. However high or low the compensation, neither a paycheck nor a single role constitute a complete adult life. Real adults have more than one social dimension to them.

One role might be the first, last and only thing some people have going for them, however. Social illiterates often define themselves, their lives and the rest of the world using the frame of reference of the one social role they take on to the exclusion of other social roles. A recent college graduate in a high-status, high-pay job might base his off-job language on his workplace vocabulary, and treat women in his supposed personal life the same way he dumps on female subordinates on the job. If the only place he gets any sort of guaranteed respect is on his job, he'll work overtime at manipulating others off the job into feeling inferior to him the same way he does on the job. He'll try to set up every part of life to bring in the same benefits that playing the workplace role brings. The hierarchical workplace role expands to fill every part of life he can expand it into, and he naturally puts himself atop the totem pole.

Conversely, a semi-literate with minimal intellectual skills might become a bully because his lack of intellectual skills produces no benefits, whereas bullying does. He practices bullying behavior that gives him some sort of perceived payoff. The bullying role expands to fill every part of his mind, and he never tries taking on other roles, let alone an emotionally available role. While the illiterate is at the opposite end of the intellectual spectrum from the college graduate, both are bullies whose bully roles (actually a dominating social role) expands to fill the blank spots in the mind where other roles should be, but are not. Both types decided to wear one social role on all social occasions.

Roles And Emotional Availability

Human beings are genetically hardwired with the capacity to fulfill multiple roles for multiple social audiences with different behavioral expectations. Only by taking on multiple social roles for different social audiences can the individual acquire the psychological, emotional and social adaptability and breadth of experience that result in a broad-based set of emotional competencies and psychological security that being emotionally available requires. Multiple roles allow for multiple social competencies, which in turn unlock the gates of the potential for intimacy. Being emotionally well-rounded thus requires prior experience at taking on a well-rounded repertoire of social roles as a sort of training wheels for eventual self-disclosure with another person in an intimate capacity.

Conversely, making one role the centerpiece of your social self-definition hobbles your progress towards social adulthood and emotional maturity. The most common form of a one-role life is defining yourself in terms of a job role and applying whatever gives you satisfaction and social status on the job to other areas of life. You end up with a one-dimensional social identity and scale down your emotional availability to whatever level of expression stays within the limits of your job's limitations on emotional expression. You incorporate this lack of emotional spontaneity into your overall personality. This is often expressed in ways such as taking on a rigid, dominant role, attempting to subordinate others, defining relationships in job–related terms and grossly inhibited, or nonexistent, emotional expression.

Single-Role Lives Jammed Into Multiple-Role Minds

When we fail to take on multiple roles, we often wind up feeling a variety of anxieties because we fail to exercise our unused psychological capacities, just as when we become restless and irritable when forced to remain incapacitated and not use our arm or leg muscles. Someone with an arm or leg in a cast develops itches and spasms due to their failure to stretch their muscles, and someone who fails to express their capacities and repressed yearnings to take on a varied repertoire of social roles becomes psychologically itchy and irritable when their inherent role capacities are frozen are in the psychological cast of a single-role life. Multiple roles are the norm, and single roles are the abnormal deviation from the norm. Our minds evolved with the specific capacity to take on multiple social roles during the course of a day. Both the muscles and the mind need daily flexing if we are to avoid atrophy and anxieties.

The human social universe is inherently socially multidimensional. If you don't use your capacity to take on multiple roles, your capacities diminish. You become a one-dimensional parody of a person in living for a one-dimensional purpose. The tension and anxieties such one-dimensional, single-role people experience in limiting themselves makes them unsuitable for adult relationships. Their tensions and anxieties block the development and expression of emotional availability because they allow themselves no flexibility in their daily routine. They always do the same thing. Emotionally available people are spontaneous, flexible people, not character actors locked into always playing a single role.

Emotionally unavailable men not only have minds filled with tensions due to limiting themselves to taking on only one role, and lack the social skills and graces adult men should have as a byproduct of taking on varied roles for different types of social audiences. They have trouble adjusting to unfamiliar social situations, carrying on adult conversations and expressing themselves in an adult fashion. Women can sense that something is not quite right about such men early in a conversation. These deficits extend to their lack of interest in meeting a woman's needs. Their regard for women's feelings do not extend beyond lip service. Their actions speak louder than empty words. One-role, emotionally unavailable men are envious and resentful of men with more social graces than they themselves possess, however carefully they work at disguising their envy. Their refusal to take on other roles and adjust to female social audiences prevents them from developing the social skills and emotional qualities more mature men develop. A man who refuses to adapt his thoughts and behavior to women has the social sense and mental flexibility of a man who wears one set of clothing all year round, regardless of changes in the weather.

Taking on a single social role confers a particular narrow form of status on the individual who meets the social expectations of that role. The problem is that any particular form of status, regardless of how much status it confers, is just not enough to round out and smoothen the sharp edges of the personality and alleviate stress.

The human brain is specifically hardwired to function optimally – that is, function calmly and efficiently – when fulfilling multiple roles each of which confer slightly different forms of status that add up in the mind to psychological calm. Any one form of status, such as that acquired on the job or by getting good grades in school, will not fill out all the nooks and crannies of the personality.

We require dozens of different vitamins and minerals each day to maintain our physical health, and will wreck our health if we engage in a misguided attempt to subsist exclusively on a single vitamin or mineral. We also require a multiplicity of psychological-status nutrients to maintain our psychological health.

There is limited substitutability between different social roles and the status they confer. Trying to substitute non-interchangeable forms of psychological status for one another can short-circuit the personality by virtue of role-status stimulation deprivation. You can neither substitute different types of vitamins nor role-related forms of status for each other.

How One-Role Men See Emotional Availability

One-role men see emotional availability as part of the psychological headdress of a psychologically foreign tribe – the tribe of women. One-role men have no mental room for women as psychologically integral parts of their lives, and emotional availability is alien to their mindset. Women appear to them to be purely physical, sexual beings or objects, and putting on an emotionally available personal front is, at best, a form of window dressing, an inconvenience they have to put up with to obtain sexual conveniences from women, their form of simmering a culinary delicacy before ultimately beginning consumption.

Putting on a pretense of emotional availability is an inconvenience they put up with. It has no more long-term significance to them than ritualistically – and emptily – mouthing empty syllables in a foreign language that is not their native tongue. They just go through the motions to get what they want. Emotional availability is a disposable option for men who live and breathe single-role lives that preclude emotional availability, as well as for men who take on multiple juvenile roles whose central tendency is to preclude the development of emotional availability. One-role men deliberately make themselves unavailable to the social environment of emotional interchange and self-disclosure by their continuing refusal to change.

Single-Role Territoriality

One–role men have most of their self-definition wrapped up in their single social roles. Their sense of control over their lives rides on that one role, and their lives are dominated by a sort of role chauvinism. This xenophobic monomania defines the rest of the world in terms of how well pieces of the external world fit into their private mental worlds defined by their single social roles. Their sense of control over their insecure lives is defined by their one-role psychological territory, the only place where they feel important. They try to define the rest of the world and other people in terms of the territory where they have the most leverage. They are insecure because they secretly compare themselves to others who take on more than one role to define and express themselves, and don't like what such comparisons reveal about themselves and their social-emotional ineptness. Such men need to feel a sense of control, precisely because their single-role lives are precarious matters, control-wise. Relationships with women thus become modeled on whatever gives them a sense of control, meaning the sense of control they get at work, which they try to extend to male-female relationships. This sense of territoriality should be taken literally, not figuratively. If a man's self-definition and self-esteem ride on his job or in his male peer group, anything not in accordance with those roles is seen as a potential threat to the shaky foundation of his self-respect.

If you think this is an exaggeration, see what happens when you tell a street gang member that you think gangs are irrelevant or a bad idea in general. Taking you seriously would leave him without any sort of turf or psychological territory where he is either boss or feels important. You become the "enemy" when you say such things from the secure perch of your own job and your unembattled social class. Not very surprisingly, when you become the "enemy," you become eligible for all sorts of disguised attacks that don't quite seem like attacks, like being used sexually and dropped like a tub of dirty dishwater. Should their basic definition of themselves be tied to some role, saying that the role that they take on means nothing to you implies that the men in such roles also mean nothing to you. To many such men, their social role is the core of their self-definition. Such men will proceed to treat you as an enemy who shows no regard for their customs and social order.

Only Pride Holds Them Back

One-role men rule over the tiniest of kingdoms: the importance their one-role lives assume in their minds. Regardless of the supposed importance of their single social roles, many one-role men are far less important to others than their fevered imaginations led them to believe. Because their self-definitions ride on their single roles, those roles assume an unwarranted importance because they lack other roles that might provide additional forms of psychological support for their self-esteem. Single roles assume an unnatural importance in determining the self-esteem of men with bogged-down lives, precisely because they have nothing else with which to prop themselves up. Such men are tediously fanatical about defending the importance of their particular single roles and their individual importance in fulfilling these roles. They have no advantage over men who can fulfill both that one particular role while also taking on varied other roles, and back off from the social arena to retreat into ruling tiny kingdoms of the mind they rope off with whatever delusions give them feelings of unwarranted self-importance.

Men married to their single-role lives are held back from expanding their thin repertoire of roles primarily due to their pride of attachment to their socially monochromatic roles. While some pluses can be derived from taking on almost any role, the limited pluses of living to fill some single role seem magnified if that is a man's one and only source of self-esteem. If they limit their diet to hamburgers,

42

they define the world in terms of hamburgers, not more varied fare such as steaks, lobster and chicken filets. Even paying token attention to other definitions dilutes the feeling of importance they derive from fulfilling their one-and-only roles if they know that they can't fulfill those other roles. They feel insecure about their ability to handle other roles for other social audiences.

In many cases, the pride they take in their single social roles overrides their long-term best interests and objective reality. A man might continue to work eighty hours a week operating his own business, even when that business continues to lose money year after year. He gets psychological reinforcement from his peer group of other small business owners. All of those peers are also single-role self-made men whose self-definitions ride on being in control of a business.

All of them tell him "don't give up the ship," regardless of the objective merits of such action. Such social reinforcement blots out his analytical capacities, which would otherwise persuade him to try another career or to shut down a money-losing business.

Should he have no other sources of self-esteem beyond his business and the opinions of peers with whom his business brings him into contact, he may very likely prefer to go down with the ship rather than give up the social status he derives from his single social role, and when that happens, he will have no social role with which to define himself.

Workaholic Roles

Being a workaholic is an all-encompassing role that, by definition, excludes taking on or learning any other major life roles because taking on other roles prevents the workaholic from expanding the workaholic role to fill every part of his life.

The role requirements of living to work blocks the workaholic from considering and taking on roles for other social audiences other than the workplace audience. This is an insecure role that fosters the development of neuroses. Workaholism encourages stress by blocking the workaholic from taking on other roles that might allow relief from stress, further increasing emotional unavailability. If you accept the bedrock premise that work is everything, the other parts of life fall into line with this premise.

Work expands to fill the time available for it, and can become a self-sustaining addiction reinforced by the minor psychological pleasures derived from successful fulfillment of a workplace role, shunting to the side the potential for pleasures to be derived from intimate relationship roles. Workaholic dedication to work precludes dedication to emotional availability, which requires relaxation time off-stage to take on other roles. Emotional availability flies in the face of the basic premise of workaholism – living to work, rather than working to live.

Being a workaholic scales down relationships to a level that subordinates relationships to the workplace role. The workaholic's narrow outlook on life requires ingraining the workaholic role into the personality and necessarily relegating non-workplace roles, and non-workplace personality characteristics such as emotional availability and expression, to subordinate or peripheral relevance because they do not contribute to the workplace role. Workaholics just don't understand that life is a box with more than one compartment. The reality is that individuals with well-rounded role repertoires are better at both their workplace roles as well as their private roles. We work better when we take on multiple roles, which operates to ease the tensions of any one role by compensating us with the psychological status benefits of the other roles we take on. People who do only one thing all the time get stale fast.

Bureaucratic Roles

One-role men often try to carry their workplace role habits over into other parts of their lives. They are bureaucrats both at work and elsewhere. They might or might not also be workaholics. This approach makes a sort of sense from their perspective. Their jobs provide paychecks ("money says I'm a success"), deference from employees lower on the paycheck scale than themselves ("losers"), offices and office furniture ("status symbols") and opportunities to control others in order to advance their employers' interests.

The less a man has going for himself in other areas of life, the more likely it is for him to try carry over inappropriate workplace role behavior and speech into other areas of life. He feels good when he acts in certain ways at work and thinks of other parts of life as extensions of what he does at work.

To such men, all of life is a one-role bureaucratic playground. They treat people the same as they do at work, meaning badly. They see no reason to take chances on taking on new roles when good things always seem to come their way when they act a certain way at work. Why bother changing? This is the bureaucratic mindset at work.

They expect the whole world to line up to be treated the way they treat everyone at work. Their one role should fit the whole world just fine, or so they think. Bureaucracies are gigantic mechanisms operated by mental pygmies, and one-role men have small minds even on the pygmy scale of measurement.

Social bureaucrats are not emotionally available. Their single life role defines their narrow lives, and there is nothing more foreign to the mind of a bureaucrat than spontaneous individuality. They have nothing to make available to women, not even a pretense of emotional availability. In their workplace world, they assign a typing assignment to a woman and expect to be obeyed, so why not extend that principle to a sexual assignment? Emotional availability makes no more sense to them than asking a secretary whether she likes whatever assignments he gives her.

No matter what a woman says or does, such men will not change. It is a mistake to think that they will. They are just too acclimated to being boss, the one role they can fulfill, and see no reason to change. Change presents the possibility of change for the worse. Should all of a man's "friends" be work-related, that is a bad sign. His entire life is tied to his workplace definition of himself, leaving no mental space for self-definitions involving intimacy or another person.

Religious zealots are not spiritual people. They are actually a particular type of bureaucrat. They proselytize others to convert them to their system of beliefs. Once others fall under their spell, they set themselves up as sole dispensers of the The Truth. What zealots seek to do is set up bureaucracies with themselves installed as unquestioned leaders, with everybody else supposedly relegated to obedient followership.

The only possible relationship others can hope to attain with such men is some form of submissive obedience. Communication flows from the top down, and the man at the top couldn't care less what those on the receiving end think. Note that both the leaders and the followers fall into the familiar one-role pattern: one role defines every part of their lives. Emotional availability is out of the question. The emphasis is on meeting the needs of one party, excluding the two-way communication and self-disclosure that emotional availability requires.

Professional followers, meaning those who always have to first decide whether what they might consider doing is acceptable to other people in general, are not emotionally available. The more they are tuned into what everybody other than themselves might think of what they should do, the less they have to bring to a relationship. If they think other people might disapprove, they wouldn't consider doing it. Men who can't think for themselves can't express themselves because they have nothing inside of themselves to express except their concern about what others might think of them.

Egocentric Roles

Egocentric roles are roles where one person is both the performer and the primary audience. Both taking on social roles and emotional availability require some adjustment of the individual's role performances in reaction to audience feedback. Adults who do not adjust their roles and performances to different audiences wind up not getting the rewards that proper role-taking should produce. When you are your own audience, don't expect your "audience" of yourself to criticize your performance, your objective importance or your need to adjust your role performances for other audiences.

Egocentric men continue acting as they do in relationships regardless of how much women point out their problems and implore them to change. For whatever reason, they lock themselves into their egocentric role. Egocentric audiences are not objective audiences.

Egocentric men are not emotionally available. They never become emotionally available until they take on other social roles and learn that they can not go through life expecting applause from others just as they applaud themselves. Being emotionally available requires playing for multiple social audiences, which itself requires attaching enough importance to external social audiences to deem them worthy of taking on social roles for in the first place.

Being emotionally available also requires adjusting one's role behavior in reaction to audience feedback. Emotionally available men make adjustments because they acquire an inferred understanding of women as a byproduct of taking on roles when with women. Normal men can mentally put themselves in the place of the woman and see things as they do. Egocentric men can not. Taking on the egocentric role short circuits the capacity to identify with others and see themselves as others see them.

Men who fail to adjust their speech, thoughts and behavior to being with women never get into real relationships. They are too wrapped up in themselves to care. Being happy with their internal audience's opinions, they care only for external audiences that agree with them. They are not interested in the sort of emotionally expressive communications that emotional availability requires. They have no interest in any other person's emotions, identifying with them or disclosing anything of substance about themselves to others. They only go as far as going through the motions of superficial adaptation to the female audience for the purpose of sexual gratification, but they no more think or believe what they say than a parrot has the capacity to believe what it repeats in a squawk. Their interests extend only to communication that reinforces their pre-existing beliefs and self-opinion.

Their egocentricity may allow them to progress in certain fields of endeavor such as sales where sheer horsepower and lungpower can carry them along. However, they do not prosper in long-term adult relationships. Egocentric roles freeze out the possibility of taking on other roles by virtue of making one's internal audience the sole standard of reference, precluding adult social interaction and the psychological adjustments that adult relationships with women require.

Some egocentric men are dominating, some are not. Within the confines of the category of dominating men, all are egocentric. All think that they are at the center of the universe and that the galaxies revolve around them. Men who already believe that the universe revolves around them find it just a small step to attempt making others fall into line with their beliefs. Egocentricity is thus an adolescent role that freezes out the potential to take on other roles. Egocentricity remains rooted in place until modified by transforming social experiences that channel the individual's thought processes into more adult channels. Don't get involved with an egocentric man unless you want to spend your time catering to adolescent self-centered fantasies and indulgences. Egocentric men offer nothing a normal woman needs.

One-Role Men Lack Core Personalities

Emotionally unavailable men with no core personality are not quite as dumb as women might think they are. Within the confines of the internal logic and rules of their own kind, their behavior makes sense. Being emotionally available goes against the grain of the overall trend of lives set up to keep them as non-adults who refuse to take on multiple social roles and responsibilities. They might go through the motions of being adult and emotionally available, but cannot keep up their ends of conversations and relationships with emotional adults. They don't know enough about adult behavior to pull it off for an extended period of time. They are psychologically immature foreigners pretending to be natives of a country of psychological adults. As soon as they open their mouths they reveal what they lack in the tone of their voices, their lack of the full range of adult facial expressions, their unfamiliarity with adult topics of conversation and inability carry on anything but the most superficial of conversations.

When with real adults, they are outsiders looking in from the outside. The best they can be called is "superficial" and the best sort of relationships they can hope for is with similarly superficial non-adult, emotionally unavailable women. They lack an autonomous core personality of individuality that is a thing apart from the public social roles they fill. They have nothing to offer real adults.

Multiple Immature Roles

Multiple roles in and of themselves do not an emotionally available adult make. Should the multiple roles taken on be immature, juvenile or nonsensical, they will retard a man's social progress. For example, a street gang member might be a slacker on his part-time job, a good buddy to some professional criminals and maybe even try his hand at role-playing games wherein he can take on fictitious roles unconnected to reality, such as chief executioner for a medieval king. If these are the only roles he takes on, filling his time with such role-playing activities block off opportunities to learn to take on adult roles in our society and his potential to become emotionally available.

The time consumed by juvenile and nonsensical roles eats up time better spent seeking opportunities to take on reality-based adult roles. A street punk who takes on multiple immature roles victimizes himself. Such roles operate to prevent him from obtaining opportunities for learning how to take on adult roles. Immature roles, whether taken on singly or in conjunction with other immature roles, constitute at best a holding pattern in a man's life, and usually constitute a retrograde movement that pushes him further outside the orbit of mainstream society. They render him increasingly incapable of learning new roles that might equip him for jobs and relationships in mainstream society. Men lacking mature role experiences to draw on never get enough practice at being an adult to become emotionally available. They never get enough experience at practicing being adults to develop the critical mass of social experiences to become emotionally available.

Chapter Three
Why Grown Men Act
Like Little Boys

Why Certain Types Of Men Choose
To Remain Lifelong Little Boys

The stronger the bond between the members of an all-male peer group, the less such men are capable of entering into adult relationships with women. Grown men remain emotional "little boys" because their peers reinforce the idea that acting like a little boy is normal behavior, at least using the peer group's definition of normal. Their one social role is the little-boy role, which requires them to avoid taking on other roles and to avoid becoming emotionally adult. Intense peer-oriented bonds preclude the development of bonds of adult forms of intimacy between peer-oriented men and normal women. This applies to street gangs, fraternities, athletic groups, drinking clubs, lodges, gambling associates and other types of formal and informal male peer groups of all social classes and educational levels. The stronger the exclusionary bond shared by members of the male peer group, the less group members are able to trust and open up emotionally with "outsiders," meaning anyone other than themselves. The bond they share operates to bond them exclusively with male peer-group insiders. If the anti-emotional ice layers applied to a man's mind by his taking on male peer-group roles becomes thick enough, the man's mind will remain frozen in a little-boy configuration. Peer-oriented men are frozen at an immature stage of psychological development. They talk and behave in a consistently juvenile manner despite being chronological adults. Being a "little boy" is a whole way of life, not a minor personality trait. They can't have adult relationships with women because they refuse to become adults in the first place. They refuse to take on adult roles and adjust to their speech, thoughts and behavior to the expectations of women. They refuse to take on the multiple roles and responsibilities that go with being adult, regardless of social class or education.

Middle-class fraternity members bring a future-oriented outlook with them to college as a result of their upbringing, but stop developing emotionally once they fall under the influence of the adolescent behavioral norms of fraternities. The time horizon of street gangs does not extend beyond the next ten minutes, as their lack of preparation for both the job market and adult relationships show. Groups of immature males will not let one of their number get serious with a woman, because little boys do not want girls interfering with their little-boy games. Peer-oriented men don't commit because the group doesn't think it's cool to commit. The group sees no benefit in losing the allegiance of one of their number to a woman, a potentially dangerous precedent that might threaten group solidarity by inducing others to follow their example. They work to keep everybody the way they have always been.

A peer-oriented man is more interested in what his peer group thinks of him and a woman, meaning their role behavior expectations, than what he himself thinks of the woman. He really thinks that he needs permission from others to have an adult relationship. Permission will not be forthcoming for something contrary to the pervasively anti-adult orientation of an adolescent-minded male social group, even if the group members are chronologically adult. A peer-oriented man dating a woman is unlikely to develop an adult relationship with her because his peers would pressure him against anything beyond an exploitative relationship that chews up and spits out women. If a fraternity member spends "too much" time with a young woman, the others will come down on him like a ton of bricks at meal time, volleyball practice and anywhere else they can pressure him. They don't want him getting "serious" because then he won't fit into their decidedly non-adult, non-serious social group. Groups demand behavioral and psychological conformity of members as a condition of remaining in the group.

Peer-oriented group members work to keep each other at the bottom of a psychological-emotional pit of stalled development. No one in the group can be allowed to rise to an adult level of enjoyment of life that might make the others jealous or envious of his individuality and maturity, except on some superficial level such as dating a homecoming queen. Adult relationships would highlight their immaturity by having around someone involved in a real relationship.

A fraternity might encourage group "responsibility" in the sense of raking the leaves in a park each week, but there is no way that the emotional nonadults in such male peer groups can offer other their fellow nonadults anything to push them towards emotional adulthood. They can't offer others what they don't have themselves. You can't expect men such as these to become worthwhile companions. They offer women nothing to build on. You will wind up supporting their juvenile character habits, and have nothing to show for it when the game ends. No matter what you say or do, the ongoing collective influence of dozens of peer group members always outweighs anything a woman says or does. They are herd animals and their peer group is their herd.

Lower-class peer-oriented men tend to be found near the bottom of the social pyramid. They want what others have, but refuse to work as others do to get there. Their ground rule that it is socially unacceptable to work hard at much of anything, so the only way for them to move up is to take on the role of financial sponges who siphon money away from others. They displace the consequences of their self-induced motivational inaction onto the first available woman willing pick up the tab in the deluded expectation that a peer-oriented man only needs to "meet the right woman" to get his act together. Women must realize that anything and everything a peer-oriented man does is simply a prop for his peer-induced central life goal of avoiding adult responsibilities and maturation.

There are differences between social classes, but only in the manner in which such behavior is expressed, not the underlying motivation behind the behavior. Lower-class gang members get their girlfriends to pick up their slack. Middle-class fraternity members get both their parents and girlfriends to pick up their versions of slack. Peer-oriented men of any social class can not handle adult relationships that presuppose two people being adult enough to put their personal desires and emotions above the expectations of the rest of the world.

Their peer groups give members permission only for short-leash emotional relationships, usually meaning short-term sexual relationships guaranteed to go nowhere, and seasoned with liberal doses of alcohol to loosen up their inhibitions and turn off whatever adult parts of the brain they might develop by accident.

The Peer-Oriented Mentality

The earlier in life that a male tunes into his peer group as his primary reference source for socially acceptable behavior, the harder it becomes for him to later become socialized to think and act in an emotionally adult manner. Getting too much early-life practice at being peer-oriented blocks men from choosing more adult options for relationships later in life. It becomes progressively harder for them to shake off their early social programming and learn new types of social roles suitable for adult male-female relationships. They miss out on the early learning experiences about relating to and understanding women they might have had were they not so tightly involved with their peer groups.

Peer-oriented boys look to other young males their own age, rather than to their parents and teachers, for answers to how to get through life. Peer-oriented boys and men look first to the reactions of those in their peer group to determine what others consider acceptable behavior, despite the reality that peer-group definitions of acceptable behavior are continually changing on a minute-by-minute basis according to the shifting sands of the random whims of the group.

There are no absolute standards of reference. When a young male looks to similarly clueless peers for answers, their answers require him to scale his behavior down to the lowest possible common denominator of conformity to group expectations. If it's not acceptable peer group behavior, it's not acceptable individual behavior. They work together to keep all of the group members at equally low levels of social and emotional conformity.

Becoming peer-oriented early in life reinforces the difficulties of developing contrary autonomous traits later in life, because such individualistic traits go against the grain of a long-standing peer-oriented mentality. Making an individual decision to plan for a specific professional career, as opposed to accepting the group consensus on whether planning for a career is acceptable, is an unlikely break from the pattern for a lower-class peer-oriented man.

Planning for a career path that represents a departure from the consensus within a fraternity, such as becoming a medical missionary, is an unlikely break from the mold for a middle-class fraternity member. Nothing in their peer group socialization would lead them to contemplate such outcomes. Street gang members also miss out on acquiring the education and work ethic values prized by the larger society and women seeking mates in refusing to take on roles other than those approved by their fellow gang members.

There are exceptions, such as those who pick up social skills, a work ethic and middle-class values before joining the peer group. Middle-class fraternity members, for that matter, often coast through life on what their parents pumped into their heads before they joined their fraternities. Should peer-oriented adolescent personality traits become embedded in the personality early in life, adult standards have nowhere to take root. The cumulative inertia of maintaining adolescent traits prevents men from becoming future-oriented psychological adults capable of taking on different social roles in their private and public lives. Unable to consider taking on roles other than those for which their peer groups condition them, they become increasingly unable to move on into psychological adulthood.

Should the bond between male peer group members be based on some negative or abusive characteristic, such as hazing, alcoholism, gambling, physical aggression, juvenile behavior or criminal activity, the group reinforces such characteristics in members by means of ongoing social pressures to practice such behavior, in addition to reinforcing emotionally juvenile behavior. Abusive male peer group activities add nothing worthwhile to male-female relationships, and men who practice such behavior become increasingly unsuitable over time for honest adult relationships. Young men who take their cues for life from psychologically adolescent peer groups become well-adapted for life within their peer groups while simultaneously becoming ill-adapted for a future in the larger society.

Peer-oriented groups circle the wagons, close ranks against the society outside their territorial gates and set up their own sets of internal sets of values to guide their private little tribal subcultural societies. Some peer groups have values that the larger society values, while others do not. Compare the cases of fraternities and street gangs. Neither expands the emotional horizons of members beyond what was in their heads before they joined their male peer groups. The purpose of both is to enforce conformity to group behavioral ideals and block out the potential for real relationships with women.

Fraternity members tend to come from the middle classes, and bring middle-class values with them, but rapidly absorb the fraternity's group norm of sliding along and doing as

59

little as they can get away with. Nobody wants to hire men who appear to be too peer-oriented to study or develop a work ethic, so fraternities get around this by means such as collecting files of old exams to make up for the lack of true academic diligence on the part of their members. The group norm is that it's okay for members of male peer groups to reject adherence to the behavioral norms of the larger society and deceive those outside the peer group, because only those inside the group's territory merit respect. Fraternity members tend to wind up in jobs where the ability to fit into a social group and socialize is valued, as in a firm where fraternity alumni rule the roost and intense socializing with the like-minded is the norm. They do less well where the ability to think for yourself and take independent intellectual action is the coin of the realm.

Peer-oriented men of every social class venerate the group ideal of always taking the easy way out, trying to slide by in life with as little effort as possible and getting someone outside of the group to pick up the slack. Stable, ongoing adult relationships reek of the unacceptable values of emotionally adult society, and peer-oriented male groups disapprove of anything beyond superficial relationships. Real relationships require effort, not sliding by. Serious, fifty-fifty relationships might induce men involved in such relationships to become psychological adults, leaving the envious peer group deprived of one of its' conformist tentacles.

Saying that it is the woman's job to make the relationship work is part and parcel of the peer-oriented mindset. Peer-oriented men believe they don't have to work at relationships or much of anything else if they can string somebody else along to do it. Saying that someone else has to carry the load for two people is a classic symptom of peer-oriented emotional unavailability.

Peer-oriented men are not psychological adults. They are psychological little boys who happen to look like grown men. Their attitudes towards women are juvenile because such attitudes fit in with their overall adolescent approach to life. You cannot expect men who look down on intellectual pursuits, meaning using your mental capacities to think for yourself, and make a cult of doing as little as little as possible in relationships - and elsewhere - whenever they can get away with it, to act any other way. The emotional futures of peer-oriented men become tediously predictable early in life because their lives are set up to allow only peers with similar mentalities to influence them.

The more heavily under the influence of the peer group are fraternity members, street gang members, athletic team members and the like, the more emotionally distant and unavailable they are with anyone not in the group. They can't get into long-term, adult relationships because they are not adults in the first place. There is less to them than meets the eye.

Peer-oriented men condition themselves to avoid thinking independently and to continue acting like juveniles for no reason beyond the juveniles who surround them expecting them to act that way. They feel their strength is in their numbers, and that the group is never wrong. Not very surprisingly, men who get their basic ideas about women from adolescent-minded peer groups see sex and relationships as entertainment. How else would you expect emotional adolescents to see it? The other parts of their lives are oriented around living up to group expectations and not having to grow up. Nothing in their environment pushes them to mature emotionally, while several factors operate to keep them exactly the way they are. Their outlook on sex, and, by extension, the women with whom they engage in sex, is adolescent from beginning to end. There's simply no way adult attitudes can develop in peer-oriented minds. Adult men think for themselves, which includes thinking your own emotional thoughts as well

A fraternity member who announces in his freshman year his plans to get married that year will not be in the fraternity for long. The same goes for a street gang member. Their actions show a lack of dedication to the group and a lack of deference to group social pressures. This peer-oriented "group-is-everything" mentality includes the notion that there no such thing as intimacy or privacy for group members. Whatever intimate activities peer-oriented men engage in with women, such activities become the public property of the group.

This means they feel free to discuss every supposedly intimate detail with other group members. Peer-oriented men who think nothing is private can't be trusted in other departments of life. You can not expect emotional availability from such men. Getting involved with a peer-oriented man automatically and inevitably means you get involved with all of the other members of his group, meaning that women become a sort of community property.

This behavior is the male version of the childish behavior certain types of insecure women engage in, in feeling that a relationship is not really right until they have discussed it with their girlfriends and obtained a consensus from the other women about the propriety of the relationship.

Peer-oriented men are little boys who always act out a role for an unseen audience of other little boys. They refuse to learn to take on any role other than the role of little boy who won't grow up.

Peer-induced conformity in the lower socio-economic classes often results in a lack of interest in formal education, failure to prepare for job market roles, failure to develop proper work habits and locking the personality in an outwardly unemotional mold. Such men develop disrespectfully juvenile attitudes towards women they maintain long after they cease being chronologically juvenile. In middle-class male peer groups such as fraternities, peer group members have typically been raised in higher income classes than gang members, and prepare, however slothfully, for real careers, but still develop and maintain juvenile attitudes towards women and long-term relationships.

Gang and fraternity members alike keep their peer-oriented group mentality long after leaving those groups. Athletes, gambling associates, drinking partners and other sorts of male peer groups share a similar group mentality: when the group sets low behavioral expectations for members in relationships, the opinions of outsiders become irrelevant. The greater the individual's allegiance to the group, the smaller the share of mind left by the group for adult relationships with women. They are just too busy working overtime at staying juvenile.

Status, Self-Esteem And Personality

Status is our society's shorthand designation for education, steady jobs and stable incomes. Normal women want to have stables lives with stable men, and things that correlate with social status usually operate to make relationships somewhat stable, predictable and enjoyable, at least economically. Having the trappings of social status does not automatically make a man emotionally available. Having a steady income does not guarantee that a man is mature, understands women or that he will adjust his behavior when with a woman. However, the lack of status increases stress and can prevents men from relaxing enough to open up emotionally.

Men with status are usually relaxed about life and relationships. A man who goes to his office job every day, brings home a regular paycheck every two weeks, does not have to worry about food and rent and has his weekends free is in a position to be sufficiently relaxed about himself to enter into adult relationships. No major sources of anxiety or tension in his life impede his expression of adult emotions. Such men don't need to be defensive about what they are. Men who get the rewards of status become both more affable companions and less likely to fill up with the frustrations, rage and low self-esteem that go with low social status, not because they are intrinsically better people, but because their social programming steered them away from life situations where high levels of stress and frustration that interfere with participation in adult relationships can be expected.

Of course, having social status does not in and of itself ensure that a man will not have emotional problems that make him unsuitable for adult relationships. Plenty of men with high incomes and high social status have drinking problems, personality disorders and abusive tendencies.

In general, however, men with status are less likely to have certain types of life-situation problems that create continual high anxiety. Men who don't have to worry about where their next meal is coming from have less bottled-up rage about their lot in life than men who really don't know where their next meal is coming from. The higher your self-esteem, the better you feel about yourself. People who feel good about themselves can afford to be emotionally open and generous with others.

Low-status, low self-esteem men are often social illiterates filled with rage about their lot in life. They are often enraged about not being unable to control women as well as about not having the social skills they might have developed as a byproduct of cumulative experience in unstructured interactions with women. The psychological byproducts of their problems usually render such men ill-equipped for adult relationships. They are looking for targets onto whom they can funnel their frustrations, not companions in intimacy.

Peer-oriented men in the lower socio-economic classes are usually unable to acquire the trappings of status. They set up their lives in ways that prevent them from getting ahead in a society that values independent thinking, formal education and good work habits. Many types of peer-oriented groups actively discourage members from developing such "straight," mainstream-society personality traits.

Peer-oriented men have to push uphill to get women to accept the notion that their peer-oriented forms of status, meaning loyalty to group ideals, conspicuous consumption, avoiding work, avoiding education and using physical aggression to attain social ends are acceptable substitutes for education, a steady job, a stable income and a pleasant personality. This is not adult behavior and should neither be respected nor regarded as acceptable adult behavior. The peer-oriented mindset blocks men from becoming psychological adults because being peer-oriented boils down to refusing to grow up and take on multiple roles such as husband, worker, father and the like. Their one social role is the little-boy role, which requires them to avoid taking on other roles and becoming emotionally adult.

Fraternity members bring with them the education and socialization they acquired before joining the fraternity, but fail to mature emotionally beyond what they were before joining the fraternity, and even develop new forms of immaturity while in fraternities. They may acquire social status, but their emotional maturity does not match their status-seeking facility. Lower-class street gang members start out at a lower level than middle class fraternity members, do nothing to move themselves up the ladder and usually remain at the starting gate of status-seeking.

They often turn to what their peer groups condition them for: lives of crime. Street gang member tend to come from the lower classes and get around their lack of a work ethic by committing crimes, both while in gangs and afterwards. They claim to have no interest in the forms of status that white-collar society offers. However, gang members are interested in the opportunities the larger society offers for conspicuous consumption, such as spending a large part of their disposable incomes on flashy clothing, cars and the like. Note the emphasis on consumption and spending, not the dirty work of taking on a productive adult role to acquire the financial means which makes consumption possible.

Social Status And Rage

Men are biologically programmed to seek status, meaning positive evaluations of themselves from other people, though the particular others they seek this from can vary widely. Feeling we have status actually creates physical changes in our minds and bodies, releasing serotonin into our bodies, a hormone that engenders pleasurable feelings and creates a peaceful, relaxed state of mind conducive to self-esteem. Conversely, the absence of status reduces our serotonin levels, removing hormonal inhibitions against physical aggression and allowing frustrations to spill out.

Men compete with other men for social status, and the trappings of social status are the means they use to attract women. Women who are attracted to men with the trappings of status sense that such men offer some prospect for stable relationships, in the sense that having a steady income reduces one possible source of uncertainty in life. Low-income peer-oriented men are at a disadvantage in modern societies in trying to attract women because they have little to offer the job market, our principal arena for male-on-male social status competition. Lack of status leads to low self-esteem, and low self-esteem in turn leads to rages about a world that does not cater to their whims. Their peer group always gave them automatic self-esteem, and they become enraged when the peer-group delusions with which they have led themselves on do not automatically translate into the good things of life in the world outside their peer groups.

Blocking themselves off from legitimate means of attaining status due to refusing to develop work habits, go to school and take on the multiple roles consistent with being an adult means their only means of attaining status and self-esteem is illegitimate means, including physical aggression. Anybody and anything that reminds low-status, single-role, peer-oriented men of what they do not have enrages them. Remember that these men are socialized primarily for life within adolescent-minded peer groups that look down on education, steady jobs and adult relationships, all of which produce positive feelings in those enjoying them. Physical aggression is often the only means of attaining status for men who decide to let their peer groups set the ground rules for their lives, and there are all too many women who are attracted to men with ill-gotten means. Another peer-oriented definition of status is the ability to impregnate women. Anyone whose definition of manhood consists of the tally on his scorecard for impregnating large numbers women is of no interest to any normal woman. If he has a scorecard, it's all just a game to him, and you're just a part of his playing field.

The greater the degree to which a peer group controls a man's mind, the less there remains for adult, emotionally available involvement with a woman. Being an emotional adult is tied to a particular society's definition of what makes a man an adult, and lower-class peer-oriented men offer little to the larger society. Boxing themselves in at every turn because they choose to remain peer-oriented makes them prone to rages. Frustrations and emotional unavailability mount as they live with the consequences of bad choices made under the influence of their peer groups. Their economic prospects are bad, and their prospects with women are even worse precisely because their job prospects are so bad. Peer-induced adolescent refusal to learn to take on multiple roles as a means of becoming an adult results in both vocational and emotional inadequacies, including emotional unavailability.

Low-income peer-oriented men are not psychological adults. They are psychological, emotional and, often, financial carnivores who must consume others because the overall trend of their lives is to shirk responsibilities and avoid maturing or changing. Their survival requires consuming others, because they often cannot make it on their own, given the ground rules they have chosen to live by. They are incapable of having adult relationships because they are neither adult nor capable of bypassing their peer-oriented social programming to become independent adults. They don't care about long-term relationships or what they do with women. Their relationships are predestined to go nowhere, so they have no reason to care about the quality of their relationships.

This is the inevitable result of a peer-oriented character structure that prevents them from taking much of anything seriously other than maintaining juvenile standards of behavior. They become filled with envious rage in seeing others enjoying their lives in ways that they made it impossible to attain themselves. They take out their rage in everybody in sight except themselves. Their inability to control their anger is yet another adolescent trait reinforced within adolescent peer groups. Their rage causes the larger society to look down on them, seeing it as additional evidence of their adolescent inability to adjust their behavior to varied social audiences with differing behavioral expectations.

Jealousy And Control

Men develop low-self esteem when little in their lives makes them feel good about themselves. A man with little education, poor work habits and an unsteady income faces an understandably uncertain economic future and has good cause for worry. Regardless of the ultimate cause of their frustrations, having frustrations about one's social status and inability to control life's course life inevitably leads to a desire to control somebody or something as a substitute for lack of control over one's own life.

This desire for control can take on various forms. Some peer-oriented men become playboys who take out their frustrations on women in general, using every woman they meet as sexual chessboard pieces, as can be seen at fraternity parties or gang orgies. Some become alcoholics who attempt to simply wipe their mind clear of their frustrations by chemical means, a form of control over one's self. Some express their frustrations against women and children, a form of control, because such victims are statistically less likely to be able to fight back than men. Still others settle for verbally abusing women, trying to propagandize a woman into lowering her self-opinion to a level below her victimizer, allowing the victimizer to feel a sort of superior. Regardless of the form in which they express their mental problems, their aim is always to blot out from their minds the results of their lies, mistakes and incompetence and project their problems onto someone else. This is how they pretend to have status. Making somebody else the target for their frustrations and bottled-up aggression diverts their attention away for a moment from the real-life problems with which they refuse to deal think about.

An aging former fraternity jock with a string of unsuccessful relationships behind him will explode at others due to his failure to understand women, identify with them and use that understanding as a basis for adjusting his speech and behavior when with them. All he really wants is the sexual fringe benefits he imagines happily married men enjoy while wanting nothing to do with the changes men have to go through to merit such perceived fringe benefits. He wants to maintain his peer-oriented frat jock mentality throughout life by manipulating emotional adults into catering to his whims. When it doesn't work the way it worked in college, he explodes in adolescent rage whenever people laugh in his face and walk away. What works in the male college peer group does not work with emotionally adult females. Peer-oriented men never understand that relationships are two-way streets with no room for grown men with one-track adolescent minds and attitudes.

Possessive jealousy is a common neurotic personality characteristic common among peer-oriented men. Losers seek to control others' lives as a substitute for the lack of control they have over their own lives. The lower on the social scale a man is, the more obsessive his desire to control the woman in a relationship. Because he has no control over the rest of his life, controlling a woman is his idea of status. This desire for control is due in part to his fanatical insistence on remaining peer-oriented and psychologically adolescent. Putting huge amounts of energy into maintaining such neuroses is another symptom of their severity. The real problem is that an adolescent, peer-oriented mindset blocks off the prospect of change should change be inconsistent with remaining psychologically adolescent. All of a peer-oriented man's energies are channeled into keeping himself and his problems exactly the way they are, expecting everybody and everything else in the world to contort themselves around him and his demands.

Lower-class peer-oriented men want to control every part of a relationship. A street gang demands unlimited loyalty from its members to a degree that necessarily precludes adult male-female relationships. The individual street gang member similarly demands unlimited loyalty even from women in short-term relationships. He's been socialized to see control as the norm for relationships, using his own relationship with his gang as a model. You can not expect anything better from peer-oriented men. Once again, the template for their relationships is what goes on in their peer groups. In relationships with women, peer-oriented men take on the role of the group as a whole while mentally slotting the woman into the role of group member subject to his control.

No matter how much a low-income peer-oriented man tries to hide it, he knows that he has second-rate social status according to the standards of mainstream society. Low status means little or no leverage over others to get what he wants. He knows he is skating on thin ice in adult relationships. The woman might meet someone of higher social status sporting more mature attitudes tomorrow and dump him without a second thought. This is a minor disappointment for a middle-class man, but the ultimate insult to a lower-class peer-oriented man. He has no other source of self-esteem open to him other than controlling a woman. Peer-oriented men want victims under their control, not companions. Their frustrations double when victims refuse to be victimized. At the far end of this social spectrum are criminal gangs who kill their wives and girlfriends simply because the gang tells them to do so. Their group social programming makes them unable to identify with anyone outside the gang, particularly women.

Peer-oriented men are possessive. They try to stop "their" women from associating with other men because they don't want women comparing them to men who might have more of the trappings of status than they do. Peer-oriented men try to keep every aspect of the relationship under lock and key to avoid losing what little influence they do have over a relationship. Such relationships are relationships only in name. They do this because, knowing they are on thin social ice, they have nothing to gain from a woman having freedom of association to migrate to greener pastures. They are jealous because they can't take the heat potential competition might bring. They do everything possible to prevent the woman from having opportunities to meet other men or do anything of any kind that might distract them from being under the peer-oriented man's control. From the peer-oriented man's viewpoint, relationships equal control, not two-way communication or emotional availability. Peer-oriented have a lot to hide, so they see self-disclosure as loss of control.

Peer-oriented men often see women as emblems or trinkets of status, not as independent individuals with whom they can identify. They see women as objects to be controlled as a means of attaining status among other men. Women are the sexual status symbols of peer-oriented men, no different than a car they don't want other men touching, a status symbol to be shown off to other men. They become jealous when "their" women date other men because they see "their" women as "their" property or territory, as if someone else were to drive off with their car. Note the similarities to a street gang or fraternity's definition of territory or "turf. " When "their" women date any representative of an "enemy" camp, such as a member of another male peer group, or, even worse, a man of a higher social class, their jealousy becomes even worse. They hate having outsiders muscle in on their "territory."

Should you tell peer-oriented men that you expect something better than control games from a relationship, you can expect them to fly into rages because no other parts of their lives are under their control besides the women in their lives. Catering to a woman's needs equates with loss of control and, by extension, loss of status among other men. Such rage is irrational because they are irrational and do not want to see or hear anything from anybody that might dilute their control over the relationship. The name of the game is power, not what's best for the woman or the relationship. Peer-oriented men often see status solely in terms of their ability to control others, exactly what you would expect men to develop in street gang peer groups. Their definition of status comes down to who and what you control.

A lower-class peer-oriented man's ideal relationship is one where he is the both the ultimate authority and free to fly into rages and tantrums to enforce his whims. What else would you expect from someone frozen in psychological adolescence? You can not expect anything better from men who work overtime at avoiding learning how to take on adult roles, responsibilities and habits. Threats and physical aggression are the frustrated peer-oriented man's substitutes for education, social status and self-control. To a lesser extent, you will also find that middle-class peer-oriented men feel the same frustrations, but middle-class men typically channel their frustrations into forms considered acceptable within their social class, such as manipulating women instead of threatening them. The motive behind their behavior remains the same as with lower-class peer-oriented men: control.

Steer clear of peer-oriented men, whatever their social class, unless you want to invite abuse into your life. The ability to abuse is their substitute for their failure to take on multiple roles and learning to become an adult. Never having learned to become adults, they don't act like adults, least of all in relationships. They expect women to adjust to them, not the other way around.

Peer-oriented men are socialized in adolescent peer groups, and go through life obsessed with "what other people think" of them. That is one of the few forms of status their peer groups have socialized them to regard, and to seek to extract from others. They apply these adolescent peer-group standards to all social situations, a common sign of the one-role mind's inability to adjust to the larger world outside the peer group.

They go into rages when people do not respect them or take notice of them, because that is what other members of their peer group have always done for them. The less they offer the larger world, the more hostile and defensive they become, and the more they take out their rage about their treatment in the job market on any opportunistic target that presents itself, such as a female companion. They just don't get it that dancing to the peer-group's tune leads nowhere.

Peer-oriented men are often obsessed with getting other people to take notice of them, defer to them and "respect" them, despite offering little that others see as worthy of respect. Middle-class fraternity members often like to point to their fraternity membership as proof that they deserve respect regardless of what they are individually. This is one form of proof that they think of themselves as undifferentiated, interchangeable members of a group rather than as individuals who need to be checked out on a case-by-case basis.

College administrations often make tacit use of this definition, basing decisions on allowing fraternities to continue to exist using the benchmark of the grades of the fraternity as a whole as proof of the sort of group mentality and behavioral expectations that fraternities foster.

Secure And Insecure Men

Men become emotionally available as a byproduct of identifying with others, learning how to deal with others, acquiring communications skills and gradually learning how to open up emotionally as they come to feel good about themselves and their slot in society. Preparation, or mispreparation, for different sorts of social environments either enhances or reduces emotional availability, depending on how well it prepares men to fit into a particular society or environment and adjust to different types of people. The greater the mismatch between a man's upbringing and his environment, the less likely it is that he will become emotionally available. The lack of communications skills useful with varied social audiences is one outcome of failing to have taken on multiple roles.

Autonomous men who adapt to the societies they live in are less likely than peer-oriented men of any race to develop neurotic personality structures that interfere with emotional availability. The general trend of their lives equips them to live and work in society and feel secure enough about being what they are to develop an adult sense of personal security about opening up in relationships. Lower-class peer-oriented men set up their lives in ways guaranteed to make them ill-adapted for both relationships and the job market, knocking over the first dominoes in a long chain of social dominoes, leaving them with character structures as ill-suited for adult relationships as for the job market. Middle-class fraternity members may be better adapted for the job market, but are ill-suited for adult relationships to the degree to which they are peer-oriented.

Men who work to become fine-tuned to the requirements of workplace environment tend to do best in attaining the forms of status available in our society, and consequently have low levels of psychological stress due to attaining some measure of status. Independent, autonomous men don't have to prove anything to others if they feel that they have proven it to themselves. By contrast, peer-oriented men become defensive and emotionally closed because they worry that others will find out what they are really like and put them down if they open up emotionally. They control relationships because only by being both in control and emotionally unavailable do they feel have any measure of security. They see communication and self-disclosure as problems, not an opportunity for exploration of new psychological territory.

Secure men feel less need to dominate relationships than insecure men because they are confident enough to not see every little thing a woman does as cause for going into a rage. They are more likely to respect women because they do not see respect for others as depriving themselves. They are less likely to become violent because they have a lot of practice in competing for society's rewards on terms other than physical aggression. Being autonomous, vocationally competent and socially skilled as a result of having taken on multiple roles is the most likely route towards developing enough inner security to be comfortable with being emotionally available.

Chapter Four
Roles, Social Instincts
And Commitment

Method Acting And Emotional Role Prisoners

The better you get at filling any role, be it good, bad or indifferent, the more thoroughly it will permeate your personality and influence your minute-by-minute speech, thoughts, actions, emotional availability and even your mental stability. Even should a role be forced on you by circumstances, and not be a role you take on by choice, it still leaves a lasting mark on you as you practice it more and more. The more you act out any role, the deeper the groove it wears in your mind by virtue of repetition.

This applies to both regular folks as well as professional actors. Actors have lives and personalities separate and distinct from the roles they play. An actor takes on roles such as spy, businessman or whatever, but does not really live the role in life off-stage, however convincingly he might fill out the role during the film's production. He simply plays the part the director and producer expect of him, cashes his check, drops that role into his memory box and goes on to fill other roles in other films. The movie audience is his secondary audience, and they vote their approval of his performance by box-office receipts, a form of financial applause for his role, as well as by word-of-mouth recommendations that operate to enlarge the audience for his role.

The psychological changes that method actors and actresses undergo in filling a role illustrate how taking on a role contrary to your basic nature can change you for better or worse. Method actors often immerse themselves to the saturation level in studying for a role. An actor playing a prisoner might visit jails, talk with convicts and ex-convicts, stay in a cell for a while and read books about prison, all in an effort to "get into" a role and get a feel for the role. This means he learns enough about the role to fill in the emotional and motivational blanks required to take on the role on his own. He develops a mental warehouse full of memories of emotional reactions to his preparatory experiences. He draws on these emotional memories to enhance his emotional expression in acting. This makes for deep involvement with a role, because immersing oneself in a role and constantly thinking about it allows an actor to mentally fill out the role as if he were actually living it. He understands everything about it inside out.

Method acting makes for good films with gripping acting, but also leads some method actors and actresses to develop psychological problems after they finish shooting their films. It's hard to shake off a role you've worked hard to make into an integral part of your personality. Even the best method actors have wound up in psychoanalysis as a result of making their roles too much a part of themselves. If the best actors and actresses can wind up as emotional prisoners of their roles in taking on what they knew all along to be fictitious roles, the average man who takes a real-life workplace role or other social role too much to heart can hardly be expected to turn out much better. The psychological byproducts of playing any major role produces unintended spillover effects that can carry over into other areas of life. Anyone who takes on a role runs some risk of becoming a prisoner of whatever role it is that they take on.

Method actors create reservoirs of emotional experiences to draw upon for use in acting. Should they want to express on stage how they feel when all alone in a cement prison cell in the middle of the night, they draw upon, and recreate, their emotional memories of how they felt when sitting in an actual prison cell as part of their role research. They create this emotional reservoir by going out and having experiences they add to their personal database of experiential emotions. Without such experiences to draw upon to guide them, the actors cannot act convincingly.

Similarly, a man cannot act in an emotionally available way with a woman without prior emotionally exploratory experiences to draw upon to guide and adjust his emotionally expressive behavior and interactions. Being emotionally available requires an experiential database of previous emotionally expressive experiences a man can draw upon to help him express himself in the here and now. Being emotionally available is a learned behavioral capacity, no different in that respect than learning to speak a foreign language. Men gradually learn to do things as byproducts of real-life experiences. The greater a man's cumulative social experiences with women, the greater the likelihood of him developing an inferential understanding of women's thoughts and needs, and adjusting his speech, thoughts and behavior to meet their needs and expectations when in intimate situations with compatible women.

Women can tell the difference between men who have made an effort to tune into identifying with and understanding women and those who have not. How such men think of women is plainly evident in their tone of voice, manner of speech, facial expressions, how they touch women and a thousand other little things. Men gradually learn to behave in this manner as they make the effort to identify with women and fine-tune their speech and behavior to being with women. Men who refuse to make the effort to identify with women and adjust their behavior accordingly are unlikely to ever become emotionally available.

Becoming emotionally available just can't be done overnight, and a man who thinks so reveals his emotional superficiality. A man who spends his time identifying with, and trying to understand, the men with whom he socializes, while making no corresponding effort to identify with and understand women, will find his lack of success at establishing long-term relationships corresponds closely with his lack of effort to understand women. What a man gets out of a relationship depends on both what he puts into his relationship as well as what he brings to a given relationship from his previous relationships. A man who spends his life in a foreign country and makes no effort to learn about the locals gets exactly what he deserves, precisely because his inaction makes no other outcome possible. A man who spends time with women and makes no effort to identify with them and develop an inferential understanding of their needs and expectations can expect the same.

Method actors must have emotional experiences to draw on if they are to express such emotions on film. We all must similarly have certain types of prior exploratory role experiences that elicited emotional reactions within us, or else we will not have the range and depth of emotionally expressive experiences necessary to fill out the breadth and depth of role of being emotional availability, at least not immediately. When we lack previous experience to draw upon for guidance, we can not call it into being on the spot. Emotional availability develops slowly, like other learned abilities, and getting there requires trial-and-error.

Self-disclosure is a large part of being emotionally available. It develops gradually, as men accumulate experience at disclosing different parts of themselves to various social audiences in the course of filling varied social roles. They get better at self-disclosure as they find that they are accepted more often than not in filling different roles with women. By contrast, a one-role man who is rejected for being what he is in his one-and-only role has no other outlets where he can develop his capacities. He allows himself no alternative means of developing those emotional capacities outside the boundaries of his single social role. Those other parts of his personality remain fallow and undeveloped.

One-Role Character Actors

One-role men are the character actors of the emotional landscape. Character actors are actors and actresses who typically play a particular type of one-dimensional role in varied productions. Their roles tend to be limited in expressive scope. While the stars and costars of productions typically express a broad range of emotions in the course of a production, character actors usually play only one narrow type of role with limited expressive scope: criminal, drug addict, martial arts expert and the like. They specialize in one thing, and only that one thing.

Character actors are the dramaturgical equivalents of one-role men. Their role-playing talents do not allow them to take on a multiplicity of roles. They are at the opposite end of the spectrum from those who star in their own lives. They are not socially adaptable and fail to adjust their thoughts and behavior women in general or one woman in particular. Being frozen in a single role stunts their development of social competencies and their capacity for self-disclosure. Living to fulfill only one role blocks them off from opportunities to take on different roles and practice self-disclosure in low-pressure social contexts.

One-role men are not the place to look for social versatility, self-disclosure, spontaneity and adaptability to meeting your emotional needs. A woman who gets involved with a man with a one-role mentality will not change him. You can neither make a character actor nor a one-role man into a star, either on stage or in real life. For that matter, one-role men are not good for much of anything requiring fine-tuning themselves to different types of people in varied social environments. They can't offer women forms of emotional expression that derive from capacities they don't possess in the first place. They are not the stars of their own lives, and only men who star their own lives can offer the wide range of expressive capacities that meet a woman's needs for emotional expression in their intimate companions.

Why We Are Social Animals

We are not a race of lone wolves, and would have lives little better than wolves were we to think and act like them. We are social animals because it is in both our individual survival interests and the survival interests of our species for us to be social animals. Being social animals means we flourish best in cooperation with other people, though not necessarily all other people. We are not interchangeable individuals, and specialize in different activities according to our individual capacities, and enjoy the fruits of the specialized labors of others instead of relying solely what each individual can produce on their own. We can collaborate with others on projects it is impossible for one person to do on his own, and reap the benefits of cooperation. Individuals are more likely to survive in cooperation with other individuals, since the weaknesses of any one individual can be counterbalanced by the strengths of other individuals when all collaborate. Human wolves do not collaborate, and limit themselves to what they can grab and run off with on their own.

We are emotional social animals as well, and are worst off emotionally when we live as emotional lone wolves. The benefits of being social animals are so great, and the disadvantages of being anti-social are so destructive, that some form of sociability is the choice of most people, especially couples. The emotional ties that bind couples together allow them to trust each other to each accomplish their own specialized tasks and contribute to their mutual support. Being emotionally available enhances your prospects for more complete enjoyment of the benefits of being an emotional adult and social animal and for enjoying intimate relations with another emotional adult.

Emotional availability is an informal, individualized role we are born with the capacity to learn to take on. The particular form emotional availability takes on depends on the particulars of the individual's personality. Becoming emotionally available requires us to fill in the blanks with what we infer from our prior experiences at taking on social roles to interact with others. We gradually develop the social skills needed to interact with the other sex as a byproduct of taking on multiple social roles, wherein we gradually edge into learning how to disclose intimate details about ourselves to a significant other. The social confidence and psychological relaxation that derive from taking on various roles in varied social settings indirectly contributes to allowing men to become emotionally available. Only men with some measure of confidence and security can relax their guard enough to become emotionally available with women. Men without the status-based inner calm and social adaptability competencies derived from taking on multiple roles are rarely emotionally open enough to disclose enough about themselves be seen by women as worthwhile long-term companions. Men who won't let women know what they are like never move beyond superficial relationships.

Roles As Adaptations To Social Environments

Fish are well-adapted to their physical environments. Their fins and gills facilitate their survival in bodies of water. We humans are similarly well-adapted to our physical environment. We walk about on two feet instead of on all fours, which enables us to hunt animals and gather plant food with considerable speed using the manual dexterity of our hands, another evolutionary adaptation that facilitates our survival. We similarly adapt ourselves to varied social environments such as schools, workplaces, neighborhoods and families filled with different sorts of people.

Taking on roles thus constitutes a large part of being a social animal. Roles are a form of differential individual adaptation to various social environments, and social environments are made up of human beings, male and female. The adaptation here largely transpires inside the mind, though what goes on in our minds is expressed in our speech, facial expressions and body gestures. The generalized ability to take on varied social roles is inborn and genetically determined. The details of the particular social roles we take on are learned or inferred from the people in our local social environments. Roles require audiences, real or imaginary, and audiences are the environments to which roles adapt us.

Taking on roles is a survival-related social instinct for adapting our behavior to local social environments. The ability to take on varied roles facilitates receiving benefits from the audiences for our different social roles. What works with one audience might not work with another. A one-role street gang member too cool to exert himself at a regular job will soon find himself out the door because he fails to fine-tune his speech and behavior to the requirements of his co-workers and supervisor. Role behavior appropriate for a social environment of street gang peers is grossly inappropriate for a workplace social audience. Roles are thus psychological survival equipment for adaptation to social environments filled with different types of people. What works with South Pacific Islanders does not work with North Pole Eskimos.

Being emotionally available in our society is a direct extension of this principle. Without the capacity to understand a particular woman's needs and expectations, and make corresponding adjustments of his behavior, a man will never be emotionally available. He fails to adapt to a social environment where the adaptive necessity centers around the needs and expectations of a particular woman, even if he thinks that the particular woman is compatible and meets his needs. It takes two to tango, and there is no such thing as emotional availability in the context of a relationship where one party makes no effort to understand the other. Infatuation maybe, emotional availability, no.

Most social roles are for public audiences of some sort. Some roles, however, are taken on either for an audience of one's self or an imaginary audience that exists only in the mind when the role is taken on, even should it exist in reality someplace other than where the individual is located at the time of a social role performance with only himself in attendance. For example, a man might polish his shoes each morning because his mother always made sure he polished them, and he continues this entrenched behavior even after she dies. The idea that she is always looking over his shoulder remains entrenched in his mind by virtue of repetitive role behavior. He acts out behavior for an unseen audience that is not there in reality.

Why Taking On Roles Stimulates Us

Undomesticated cats in the wild go after mice because that is their source of food. Cats evolved an instinct that makes them delight in going after mice, and so cats chase after mice even if they are not particularly hungry. Cats enjoy chasing mice because the instinct they evolved gives them an instinctual pleasure that made survival-related activities more likely to occur. People enjoy interacting with other people because we enjoy practicing, and even playing at, expressing survival-related role-playing activities specific to the human species. The key to our survival is interaction and cooperation with other people, speech is our primary medium for facilitating social interaction, and roles are a primary form of social interaction mediated by speech.

The capacity to take on roles is an instinct, and most people enjoy taking on more than one social role. We are born with the built-in, biologically hardwired capacity to take on different roles as the requirements of our social environments filled with other people might require. We are biologically hardwired to feel an instinctual stimulation from, and enjoyment of, the various roles we take on.

Conversely, not taking on multiple roles is stifling, and probably warps the personality by reason of understimulation of minds geared by evolution for higher levels of stimulation by means of taking on different roles. Men and women thus want to play varied roles, even if there is no other obvious benefit from doing so, simply because being human requires the sort of social and mental stimulation derived from social interaction in different roles for varied audiences. If sufficient stimulation is not immediately forthcoming, we entertain ourselves in other ways, such as by means of role-playing and fictitious roles. We thus enjoy taking on roles because it feeds an inborn, evolved, instinctual capacity that requires regular stretching to avoid restlessness due to understimulation.

We feel pleasure in gratifying our instincts. Instincts come with an itch, an inducement to satisfy or relieve the tensions of instinctual arousal. Instincts are inborn biological drives that function to motivate us towards some sort of thought or action to release the tensions that instinctual drives build up within us, and are usually related to some sort of survival or reproductive interest. We run from fire because our flight-from-danger instinct creates a tension that forces us to flee from the danger of fire. Sexual arousal creates a tension that sexual release relieves. We find that stimulation both in arousing some kinds of tensions and relieving them. Sex is one example, hunger is another.

We evolved as social animals for whom group cooperation was the key to survival in the ancient world, where a human lacking the natural weapons possessed by other animals had little chance of independent survival. It is not surprising that we feel pleasure from beneficial social interactions apart from their contributions to our social survival. We enjoy interacting with people because we evolved to feel pleasure in social activities, and we feel stimulation-pleasure from engaging in social activities because they are vital to our survival. The stimulation-pleasure we derive from gratifying our instincts is simply a survival mechanism evolved to make behavior that enhances the survival of the individual, the species, or both, more likely to occur because we enjoy the feelings we get from engaging in such behavior.

Different roles stretch our psychological capacities. Stretching our minds by taking on varied roles is pleasurable, just as exercising our bodies is pleasurable. Taking on roles affords us mental pleasures, and that is why we take them on in the first place. Even children take on roles such as teacher, daddy, mommy and nurse on their own initiative. Role-playing is an enjoyable way to use our energies, and is such an integral part of our endowment that even children feel impelled to try their hands (or minds) at taking on varied roles.

Roles can be wholly fictitious. Role-playing games wherein game players taken on roles such as master, slave, soldier, and so on, allow players to take on different roles with varied game-related role expectations. People play such games because these games allow them to flex their mental muscles and try out stimulating, if artificial, new forms of social relationships. Some people similarly take on different roles when conversing online just to try something new and different. It is not the particular role so much as the opportunity to try on various sorts of social hats and see how they fit, as well as running one's own flag up the flagpole and seeing if anyone salutes. The key point is that trying out different roles is stimulating because our brains have this specific capacity for both being able to take on varied roles, and to enjoy doing so, because of the survival value of being to take on different social roles in different social environments. The capacity to enjoy taking on roles is an instinct we have an itch to express. Actors and actresses make their livings taking on roles for entertainment purposes, and people watch the films they appear in because we enjoy identifying with others, even wholly imaginary others, and mentally putting ourselves in their shoes or roles. Unsuccessful films often have the primary defect of presenting characters with whom we are unable to identify. If we cannot put ourselves in the shoes of the character portrayed, or the role they fill in a film, such films will make no emotional connection with us.

Continual Adjustment Of Behavior

It is not a big step to go from adjusting and fine-tuning your behavior to suit the expectations of different social groups that get successively smaller and smaller (from nation to workplace to family) to adjusting your behavior to the smallest of social groups – the one other person who is involved with you in a relationship. Diverse social experiences tune you into acting differently at different times, meaning the fundamental concept that you can not always act the same way with different groups of people because you tune into one audience while tuning out other audiences at the same time. You still have to actually learn the details of any particular role by trial and error, of course. However, as you practice you get better at fulfilling roles and obtaining the social benefits conferred by filling roles. We all must continually probe our social environments and adjust our outwardly expressed behavior accordingly.

Observing the opposite effect helps delineate this principle. Someone who persists in acting the same with every social audience will fail to obtain the benefits of acting out roles customized for those audiences according to the degree to which he remains petrified in the thought and behavior patterns of a single role. A street gang member who attempts to apply his street gang member role to other social audiences – such as job supervisor, a girlfriend or his parents – will fail miserably in those other roles. Those other social audiences derive no benefit from him acting out his gang role for them, and they will confer no benefits on him. His boss has no use for lackadaisical workers, his girlfriend has no use for a male more closely bonded to his street gang associates than to her and his parents have no interest in the language he brings home from his street-gang peer group.

His role behavior offers his secondary audiences no benefits, and they will not give him any benefits for failing to live up to their role expectations. Eventually he will have to adjust his behavior to other audiences, as might happen when he someday moves on to other arenas of life, such as the military, and he will have to continue adjusting himself in new ways to new social audiences. Social survival requires continual, fine-tuned adaptation to different mixes of people with varied behavioral expectations in different social arenas.

How Audience Expectations Impact Men

Men take on different social roles to meet the expectations of different social audiences. Not very surprisingly, should the central tendency of their social audiences be hostile to spontaneous emotional expression and availability, men who practice taking on roles for those audiences will tend to become inhibited, repressed and emotionally unexpressive. Should you get a lot of practice at filling any particular role, you grow (shrink?) into that role until endless repetition of that role's behavior wears a deep groove in the mind. You become the prisoner of the role expectations of other people. Should you fill only one major life role, you become the character you play, an extreme version of method acting. Should a man act out a role for an audience of psychological adolescents, such as a street gang or fraternity, the nature of his audience determines the limits of his emotional availability, assuming the audience allows it to any degree at all. He becomes the prisoner of the role expectations of his audience. One common expectation is that he dedicate his life to living the one role they expect of him and not divert his energies to other roles, particularly roles that require taking on an adult role with a female audience.

You can not expect a young man, especially in his most impressionable years, to avoid taking on, and living up to, the expectations of those for whom he performs his role to obtain social approval and social status. He would not be performing for them in the first place unless he valued what their opinions of him for some misguided reason or other.

Commitment Is Individual-Specific

Commitment is individualistic behavior. A man who blocks out opportunities to get involved with many women does so because he prefers to be intensely and intimately involved with one particular woman. Men are born with the instinct to bond with women, but which particular woman a particular man chooses to bond with is a totally individual matter. Commitment is individual-specific, not generalized to "nice" women as a group. A man might be comfortable with women in general, but needs to see a lot of good reasons that speak directly to his personal interests to commit to some particular woman, and only ongoing communication will lead him there. The intermeshing of compatible personalities is many times more exacting than the proper of fit of clothing, complicated by people being in a state of continual psychological flux as they mature and learn from their experiences.

Commitment is a manifestation of increasing emotional availability with a particular woman. Emotional availability itself is a manifestation of the development of an individual core personality separate and distinct from the parts of the personality that respond to group behavioral expectations. The closer the degree to which a woman matches up with his unspoken expectations in his head is the degree to which he is likely to become emotionally available. Simply because a woman is pleasant, attractive and intelligent, does not mean that a man whom a woman thinks "ought" to commit to her necessarily will commit to her.

Men are not robots into whom women can feed generalized stimuli that automatically result in a conditioned commitment response. It takes two to tango, and a given man may prefer to tango with different sort of female social dance partner. A man may be open to commitment, but prefer to make himself emotionally available only with a particular type of woman who fulfills his individualized expectations, specifically meaning his unverbalized definition of her ability to meet his individualized multiplicity of emotional, behavioral, sexual, social and intellectual needs. No matter how much a woman thinks she has done her best to live up to her self-determined definition of being sort of woman that she thinks a man "ought" to like, any particular man can see things differently.

Most men will not specifically verbalize their mental array of needs to a woman because men see no need to let most women know much about their needs or what they look for in women. Men see no need to explain much to women in the early stages of the mating dance. They think that spelling out their innermost desires allows women to attempt to manipulate how they present themselves to men.

Men know that women are out looking for men who will commit, and many believe that women will present an inauthentic personal front and take on an inauthentic role to get a man to commit to an image of a woman that has no basis in her inner reality. Men believe that women put on elaborate acts to hook men, and are reluctant to help the women tailor their performances to hook and reel in the audience. They prefer to see what a given woman is really like without any sort of leading clues from a man.

If a man is willing to commit, he will do so – but only with a particular type of woman with whom he feels no reserve or inhibitions about commitment. If a man doesn't feel right about committing, he will not commit, period. No matter how much a woman tells a man that she – or, even worse, her girlfriends – thinks that the two of them are a perfect match will change his mind. He knows what he likes and does not care what others think he ought to like.

A frenzy on the part of a woman to extract commitment, or a rush to the altar by a woman racing her biological clock, does not constitute an emergency in the mind of a man. The infinite shadings of the subtleties of personalities are such that, even if a woman says it looks like a match made in heaven from her end of the relationship, the differences and subtle mismatchings she chooses to overlook and blot out when in a frenzy to obtain commitment are by no means blotted out in the mind of the man. What a woman sees as a microscopic irrelevancy is something a man knows he is unwilling to put up with on a daily basis over the long term.

Women often make the serious mistake of assuming that because a man is unable, or unwilling, to verbalize what he prefers, or is looking for, that his mind is an empty vessel into which a properly conniving woman can pour an image of the perfect match for him, and that image just happens to look just like her, by sheer coincidence. This is incorrect. The man maybe just biding his time with a woman who meets one-third of his total needs while being on the lookout for a woman who offers him more according to his personal standards of definition. Commitment and emotional availability are as purely individualistic as a particular key customized to fit into a particular lock. No master-key will unlock the door to commitment for one man or all men. One size or personality configuration will not fit all men.

Commitment is one positive outcome of a man being emotionally available. A man might not commit to a particular woman, however, despite being emotionally available, he might evaluate that particular woman as "nice enough" but incompatible, regardless of how the woman sees the situation. Commitment means that an emotionally available man has identified qualities in a particular woman that makes him want to dedicate his emotional energies to her and block out considering other women as candidates for emotional or sexual commitment.

Commitment is thus a byproduct of being emotionally available, with an emphasis on the individual man's evaluation of how a particular woman meets his personal needs. Just because a man is unattached does not mean he will commit to the first woman that comes along. No compatibility means no commitment. Men can be just as fussy as women in this regard.

Chapter Five
Emotions And Personality

Emotions

Emotions are instinctual forms of communication about our internal states of mind to real or imaginary audiences, including ourselves. We communicate our emotions by speech, touch, facial expressions, gestures and body language, using the human body as our medium of communication. Emotions can also be communicated by symbolic means such as writing and music. Emotions communicate, either to social audiences or to our conscious selves, our evaluative reactions to what we think and experience. Just seeing the expression on another person's face speaks volumes about how they think of us, themselves, other people or about their reaction to the impact of some external event that touches them. The ways in which a man and woman touch each other in intimate moments similarly speaks volumes about how they regard each other. We can also choose to repress emotions and keep them to ourselves.

Emotional expression is tied to our roles. Certain social roles require the expression of emotions, while many others discourage or repress all but the most formal forms of emotional expression. A prison guard's social role on the job encourages much less emotional availability than does a mother's social role. Emotional expression learned on the job is tied to some extent to the individual's degree of suggestibility, here meaning the extent to which an individual unquestioningly takes on role behavior others expect of him. The more unquestioningly a man takes on role behavior and thought patterns others expect of him in some social role, the less of an individual he is and the more the role others expect him to fill becomes his individual reality. Individuality requires having a core personality to mediate and decide which roles best serve the purposes of the individual rather than those of his external social audiences.

Emotions often being tied to social roles, they require interaction, either in the context of social roles transpiring in real life, or possibly within the context of imaginary social roles in one's head. Even an isolated individual can feel and express emotions, though they may be reactions to fantasized or wholly imaginary social experiences and people, and need not be grounded in any sort of reality-based social context. Developing fully adult emotions requires extensive real-life contact with other people. Emotions in asocial individuals remain fixated on the adolescent, or even preadolescent, level, due to the lack of adaptive interaction with others which are required to fine-tune an individual's speech, thoughts and behavior to dealing with specific people. Mature adult reactions require endless ongoing modifications and ongoing adjustments in dealing with others, such as in the tone and volume of voice used, choice of words, sentence complexity, and so on, if the speaker is to express himself on a communicative level beyond the adolescent.

Learning how to deal with others requires extensive social contact with others and a gradual, trial-and-error process of adjustment. The more adult and intimate the relationship, the greater the necessity for fine-tuning and tailoring one's speech, thoughts and behavior to the specific individual. Maturity requires dealing with people by adjusting your behavior to them, regardless of what you really think of them deep down. Adults just cannot fly into childish temper tantrums whenever things do not go their way, for example. We must tailor our speech, behavior, attire and the like to the expectations of the social audience of the present moment while tuning out irrelevant social audiences as we tune into our audience of the moment.

You can not speak or act with your employer the way you act with your spouse, for example, or even express yourself in the same emotional tone of voice. Polishing the communicative and emotional parts of your personality requires grinding down the spikes of self-centeredness associated with the lack or adjustment to living in an interactive social environment filled with other people.

Just as we must wear protective footgear when walking on sharp rocks, we must similarly adjust ourselves to social environments filled with sometimes-spiky people by coating our reactions to them with layers of fine-tuned social adaptation. We modify our emotional expression to suit varied social contexts filled with different types of people

Emotions And Cognition

Emotions are instincts found in both human beings and other animals, and are determined in large part by the operation of a specific physical part of the human brain known as the limbic system. We have some emotional characteristics in common with animals that exhibit emotions, such as dogs, but several major points of difference as well. Emotions are a form of outward physical communication about our internal states of mind in reaction to real or perceived information, events, circumstances or expectations, positive or negative. We communicate our subconsciously-generated emotions to our conscious human minds. These emotional communications spill over into our bodies, particularly our faces, which in turn express our emotions in outward physical form to others in our social environments. Speech is another primary means of expressing emotions.

The primary differences between human beings and other animals is that, at least in mature adults, our emotions have a major cognitive-rational component, and a much wider range of types of emotions, than any other animal. A dog might feel sad in immediate reaction to a death. A human being might be saddened by hearing about a medical diagnosis that, while not having any immediate, on-the-spot negative consequences, might ultimately have serious long-term consequences. The rational human part of our mind processes information and transmits the results of our cognitive evaluation to the subconscious.

A piece of paper, or a computer screen image, with a medical diagnosis encoded in a symbolic language means nothing to a dog, but means quite a bit to a human being, because our brains cognitively evaluate what we see and hear. Our brains understand more, process more and thus produce end results with more emotional implications than a dog or cat exposed to the same information on paper or computer screen.

Those animals lack the mental capacities to understand the intellectual implications of the information to which they are exposed. Emotions are thus not at the opposite pole from rational thought, but are instead linked to, and interwoven with, our rational thought processes.

Emotional Availability, Learned Behavior
And Learning About One's Self

Emotional availability is learned behavior involving fine-tuning one's thoughts and behavior to adaptively communicate and engage in emotional expression with the other sex. The more you know about adjusting your thoughts and behavior to social situations filled with other people, the better able you are to decide to whom you wish to reveal your true emotional self. When you know what you are like yourself, you have a starting point for finding compatible others.

"Knowing thyself" in relationship to others allows you to calculate and gauge your personal emotional interests and decide for whom you wish to take on – and not take on – intimate roles. The better you know yourself as a result of dealing with others and learning what sort of people you prefer to spend time with, the better you can specify and act out your preferences by focusing on seeking out only certain types of potential intimate companions.

Knowing yourself lets you determine which sorts of people are the most appropriate for commitment and decide when to make yourself emotionally available to certain other people. Learning about yourself is itself a form of learned behavior you can use to guide yourself towards further refinement of both your overt behavior and private choices.

Romance, Empathy And The Group Instinct

Romance and empathy are instinctual capacities related to the human group instinct. While the two are not identical, they do seem to overlap. Romance involves an overpowering attraction to another person that sometimes seems (at least

101

to those outside the romance) to override both the facts of the matter as well as conventional forms of logic. Empathy involves feeling for another, or identifying, in the sense of putting yourself in the place of another and seeing the world from his or her perspective.

Romance is a form of expression of the group instinct, in the sense that we are attracted to the idea of being "together" with another, often despite the reality that two people may have little in common. It is a form of initial attraction that facilitates the reproduction of the human species by virtue of bringing people together in a way that suspends their rational faculties for the moment. The simple fact of enjoying the feeling of being together seems to override all other concerns when two people are in the romantic state of mind.

Note that descriptions of the romantic state of mind bear substantial similarities to the mentality of a deindividualized audience sharing a blissfully receptive state of mind in being surrounded by like-minded others at a concert or other group experience. Just being with like-minded others at a concert tilts their mental balance towards a relaxed, receptive, group-oriented state of mind wherein individual concerns fade from mind.

Just being together with like-minded people, here meaning two people attracted to each other, makes two romantics happy, even if the fact of the matter is that they really have nothing in common beyond a mutual need for companionship. The "couple" feeling fades over time as reality-based thinking sets in and attraction fades as they learn more about how little they have in common, just as the blissful group feeling fades as the crowd disperses at the end of a concert.

Both romance and the group instinct thus seem to be instinctual mechanisms to bring people together and to instinctually enjoy being together. Romance is an instinct designed to make reproduction more likely, and thus species survival more likely, by virtue of making people instinctually enjoy being together, at least in the short run.

Empathy seems to be an instinctual cousin of the group instinct. Empathy is a form of identification with another person, and probably aided the cause of the survival of the human race early in our evolution. If you felt instinctual empathy for others, you experience and feel as they experience and feel, a more intense form of the ability to identify with others. Such a close form of identification with others made you likely to try to help them and thus aid the cause of the survival of the small human groups which were the norm for most of our evolutionary history. In the ancient world, humans had to collaborate every day to survive the predators and natural disasters, such as lack of food, all around them.

Empathy is thus an instinctual mechanism that helped both groups and individuals. Feeling empathy for another person or group can make you want to associate with them, help them and possibly even mate with them, as with a female forager-food gatherer who nursed back to health a wounded male hunter because she felt that his troubles were her troubles as well. One specialized form of empathy is that of mother for child.

A sensitivity to children's needs was beneficial to the survival of the human race, and women who did not have that instinctual urge towards sensitivity for children's needs probably left few descendants who carry that trait to this day, because their lack of that urge made them less likely to do every possible thing to help the child survive because they did not feel it as an issue of direct personal concern.

Conscience, meaning an ethical sense of right and wrong, is a higher-order intellectual function, a learned capacity involving the rational human parts of the brain. Developing a conscience derives from having been exposed to, or developed on one's own, some sort of social-ethical standards of reference or internalized social guidelines regarding right and wrong.

A conscience provides guidelines for evaluating one's own behavior and provides an incentive for taking action when ethical standards are violated. Conscience is not the same as empathy. Empathy is an instinctual capacity for feeling what another person feels. Conscience is something we learn or acquire learn or acquire over time as we are exposed to people, experiences and situations from which we derive ethical guidelines for ourselves.

Emotional Availability And Cumulative Experience

Cumulative experience means the sum total of whatever you have done in a particular area. As you accumulate more experience in almost anything, you get better at it because you develop more effective and efficient ways of doing it as you do more of it – speech, writing, sex, wood carving and so on.

Since emotional availability is a learned or acquired trait, as you have more real-life social contact and emotional or social communication with the other sex, you usually get better at communicating with them, and expressing yourself with them. At the very least, you should know more about the one person with whom you spend the most time. You try new and better ways of saying, doing and expressing things, some of which work and some of which do not, and you continue practicing the ones which work out best.

Some men do this. Men with various mental blocks against doing anything beyond the superficial do not. This explains why some people, though not all, report that as they get older, they enjoy their partners more and more. If two people are compatible and communicative in the first place, they have more to communicate about in ever-new ways as they mature and share the unfolding fruits of their maturity with each other. This is actually cumulative experience plus wisdom or judgment.

Not very surprisingly, since sex has a sizable mental component, emotionally communicative people also report enjoying sex more as they get older. This applies, however, only to people who want to benefit from their experiences and work at fine-tuning the ways they communicate and express themselves. Some people refuse to adjust and change. They just keep repeating old forms of non-adult behavior without thinking about what they are doing and how they ought to be expressing themselves, a classic sign of continuing immaturity.

It's hard to see an aging street punk, who decided early in life that women are disposable playthings, ever becoming emotionally available, though he may develop a smoother line of patter with increasing age. On the contrary, aging street punks will probably freeze themselves into their adolescent anti-intimacy, anti-change, anti-intellectual, pro-aggression mindset throughout life. Their social selves remain locked into the anti-adjustment social role their street gang peer group decided they should take on. They remain locked into this mindset even after leaving the gang, just as died-in-the-wool frat boys never really grow up, though they pretend to do so in a variety of ways. Groups exist to control individuals by applying pressures to conform to group behavioral norms, and gangs are one such group. They are instinctual conformists incapable of becoming adults. Decades of cumulative experience at being what they are freezes them into the mold of emotionally unavailable men who don't want to learn to identify with women and don't want to change their behavior when with women.

As conformity to social roles for public audiences increases its' grip on the individual's mind, the individual's ability to mentally step outside that role and make emotionally autonomous decisions about his emotional life decreases radically. Died-in-the-wool conformists are not emotionally available, in part because they worked at avoiding individualistic experiences that might have led them become emotionally available. The minds of normal men have experiences that at least point them towards becoming emotionally available, while emotionally unavailable men have only blank spots where those experiences should be. They have neither the experiences nor the motivation to change.

Emotional Availability Means Spontaneity

Being emotionally available means, among other things, having a core personality beyond the social role behavior taken on for varied social audiences. It means having a private, individual, internal mental life and personality in addition to the public-role mentality put on in taking on roles for others. One key characteristic of emotionally available men is that they converse freely and spontaneously when they are with compatible female companions of their choice. They disclose what they really are and how they feel about women. This is the opposite of the sort of speech and behavior patterns encountered in men who take on only those roles that are characterized by unemotional, formal, scripted speech patterns and topics of discussion.

This trait is particularly noticeable in men with one-role, one-track minds and lives. Their one-trick pony social role, which is often work-related, forces their personalities into boxes from they can not escape without losing whatever status they derive from fulfilling their single role. Anything with the potential to downgrade their one role gets swatted aside because change turn out to be change for the worse. There is no guarantee their status will not degrade or worsen. The prospect of change is always unsettling to one-role men, because they have no alternative sources of status and identity beyond their single roles. Spontaneity is out of the question, because living out one role twenty-four hours a day disallows anything outside the perimeter of that role. Emotionally unavailable men see everything in terms of their status and the respect they think their status should accord them. By contrast, emotionally available men speak openly and spontaneously, at least when with significant others. They have sufficient social status and social adaptability to relax and not see self-disclosure and open conversation as threats to their status.

Why are emotionally available men spontaneous? They need a break from the rigidity of the public social roles they take on to obtain the resources they need to sustain themselves and their core personalities, which emotional availability reflects. Spontaneous unscripted speech not derived from public social roles also reflects their relaxation with their social status. They are confident about their social status, which derives from the respect others accord them when they fulfill varied social roles. Their cumulative intimate experiences with women add to their confidence. They know women accept them for what they are. Even should one particular woman treat them wrongly, they do not take it personally. They just move on. They have enough cumulative confidence such that it has become a natural part of their personalities. Thus, they do not bristle at every real or imagined slight. Confidence breeds spontaneity, lack of confidence results in emotional unavailability and scripted, patterned speech derived from whatever single role status rests upon. The more rigid that single social role, the less emotional availability the man offers, because living to act out some single social role freezes out the spontaneity and casual attitude on which emotional availability depends.

Sense Of Humor And Emotional Availability

A man with a real sense of humor might or might not be emotionally available, but is probably not completely closed off to the possibility. He has some sort of foundation for developing in that direction. Emotional availability requires the capacity to see life from a perspective outside the social roles we take on and the role-expectations baggage that accompany them. A man with a sense of the absurd and ridiculous usually does not take himself, here meaning the social roles he fulfills, too seriously. If he defines himself in terms of some single social role, he is a bad bet for a relationship. He knows that much of what he does in a role, such as on a job, is simply nonsense he must spout to get through the sort of day his workplace role forces him to go through. His workplace role is not something central to his sense of self-definition.

A sense of humor involves the ability to see things from an outsider perspective, and often involves an unexpected or spontaneous viewpoint on situations or events. A man who is able to see the world, and the roles our social world requires people to take onto survive, from an outsider's perspective is likely to also see himself and the roles he plays in that manner. He has a core personality independent of his social roles. This core personality is what you hearing speaking through the medium of his sense of humor, his capacity to stand outside his social roles.

A sense of humor is an adult capacity, an aspect of one's core personality that allows one to see things from the perspective of other roles or from a perspective outside of the social universe of role-taking. A sense of humor is thus a manifestation of the internal capacity for taking on multiple roles. This adult sense of humor differs from the "humor" of a professional jokester, who is actually a one-role clown unable to consider taking on any role inconsistent with his central role of clown. His primary source of gratification is his jokester status: he is "in the know" about the upcoming punch lines of his jokes, and whereas others are not.

Certain types of humor indicate the potential for emotional availability. A sense of humor reflecting an outside-the-role perspective reflects an underlying adult mind and emotional capacities. A focus on inhumane topics such as sadism, aggression, name-calling, endless put-downs, and the like reflects a non-adult sense of humor. Some men have a sadistic sense of humor, where the point of their "humor" is to humiliate, degrade, or sneer at, others, reflecting the absence of a balanced adult core personality. Such men want to see everything and everybody in terms of a role where they are always on top and engaged in kicking other people around. A sadistic sense of humor reflects the desire to dominate others, an instinctual trait that precludes emotional availability. Sadism is an instinctual role that prevents freezes those so endowed from taking on other roles, learning new social skills and developing the capacity for emotional availability. Sadists are not emotionally available, not matter how well they mimic the emotionally normal. Sadistic humor is a means of propping up a one-role man's social status by "proving" he has status, the proof being his ability to put down others and get away with it, in part because he disguises his humor as "jokes". Emotionally available men secure in their self-esteem see no need for this under normal circumstances.

A sense of humor means a man does not take everything ultra-seriously, and can think outside of the restrictions of his roles. By contrast, a man with no sense of humor probably takes everything dead seriously. He is unable to inject elements of the unconventional derived from either his own personality or other social roles into his speech and thoughts. Humorless men are one-role men unable to see anything from outside the perspective of the one social role around which their lives revolve. They may or may not be sadistic, but are definitely dull.

The House Of Personality

An adult man takes on a variety of roles for various social audiences. They become the bricks of his house of personality. The problem is that bricks alone do not a house make. Simply stacking up bricks on top of each other just doesn't cut it. Bricks need cement to hold them together in a coherent structure, or all you have is a pile of unconnected personality bricks presenting a facade to the outside world, and nothing behind the façade.

There must be some sort of psychological cement that ties together the roles taken on for external audiences into some organized purpose chosen by the individual. Regardless of whatever sort of bricks are used to create a house of personality, somebody must live and breathe inside the house, or all you have is an emotionally unoccupied hollow shell built to satisfy external audiences passing by on the road of life. A man with nothing more to him the sum of the social roles he takes on for others is no man at all. A life lived only to impress others is no life at all.

A core individual personality assigns – or does not assign – value or importance to roles a man takes on. The standard of measurement is the value created for the individual in relationship to his individual aims and goals in life. A man lacking a core personality is simply an actor seeking applause for a string of roles he takes on for public social audiences. If meeting the needs of external audiences in strictly-defined social roles, such as workplace roles, is a man's sole standard of value, his personality deforms around living up to others' expectations.

He becomes no more than the sum of what others think and expect of him, and not what he thinks of himself and wants for himself. There is no hope for a man or woman without a core personality, Their lives always blow whichever way the random winds of their social environment blows.

Emotionally available men have autonomous identities, values and self-definitions independent of their public social roles in social settings such as places of work. Emotional availability is a part of an individualistic role they play for themselves and self-selected private audiences.

For that matter, picking one's roles and knowing when to stop playing for others and start playing for yourself is a function of having an independent, autonomous, individualized personality.

A man should add up to more than the sum of the social roles he plays for others in public. A man should take on roles for himself and private audiences of his personal choice, as opposed to taking on only social roles for public audiences such as workplace audiences. When a man's lower-level physical needs are taken care of, he should move up the scale of increasing psychological independence from both the people and things in his environment and become progressively more self-programmed in his thoughts and actions. His autonomous core personality does this programming, as opposed to public social role behavior and thoughts other people program into him. His core personality is the individualistic part of his personality that develops outside of the social-audience context, what he would develop on a desert island if he were thrown back on his own resources.

The social roles you take on can shape your life outside of those parts of life wherein you take on that role. An easy-going, lackadaisical young man who goes to law school and finds work as a lawyer might not only become an aggressive, argumentative and nitpicking attorney in court. He will also carry these traits over to other parts of his life. Everyone does this to some extent. It is a rare man who can so completely compartmentalize his life such that you get no clue from how he acts in his private life roles what he does in the other compartments of his life.

Some men like this go too far in the wrong direction. They take on the role of lawyer, they grow into the role and fill out the role to the extent that the role expands to fill out the blank spots in their personalities with carried-over pieces of the lawyer role. The role of lawyer expands to fill every nook and cranny of a man's personality to the extent to which a man lacks a core personality, and lawyers can be one-role men just as readily as men in any other occupation. One possible outcome is that one such one-role man will treat his girlfriend the same way he treats suspects in court. His courtroom personality expands to fill in the blank spots of his boyfriend personality and role. As he gets more practice at the lawyer role, and works long hours as a lawyer, the extension of the lawyer role to other parts of life becomes increasingly likely. Roles expand to fill the unused space in the personality where multiple roles should have taken root, but did not, because the man chose to not take on other roles in the first place. The single role of lawyer thus spreads out like weeds to fill all of the vacant space in his mental parking lot.

By contrast, a similarly easy-going, lackadaisical young man who entered law school at the same time as the first young man turned out quite differently, despite both undergoing the same role-indoctrination process to which aspiring lawyers are subjected. The difference is that the second man had a pre-existing core personality before going to law school. His personality thus had less vacant space into which the law-school experience could expand.

The lawyer role is just one social role the second man fulfills. He is just as professionally intense as his law-school colleagues on the job. But, once he steps out of court or his law office he puts on his core-personality hat, his authentic-self personality. He knows he must act differently with his girlfriend than in court, and developed social skills specific to dealing with women years before in taking on other roles wherein he gradually learned how to interact with women in intimate situations.

Behaving differently with his girlfriend than with suspects in court is what he does. He knows his courtroom hat is not the hat to wear in his girlfriend's living room. No matter how much he practices any one role, he knows that each role is just a hat he can put on and take off as the occasion requires, and no single role is the be-all and end-all of his life. The second lawyer is emotionally available in part precisely because he learned that he must act differently when with differing types of people.

He thus takes on multiple social roles for different social audiences. Taking on a well-rounded repertoire of roles has made him a better-rounded, better-adjusted, individual than the first lawyer, who cannot think outside of the confines of his self-chosen single social role.

Eliminating Communication
Eliminates Emotional Availability

Emotional availability requires ongoing, two-way communication about needs, reactions and feelings from both members of a couple. Whatever reduces or eliminates two-way, spontaneous, self-disclosing intimate communication automatically reduces emotional availability. A lack of communication means you don't know anything about the other person because it is not communicated to you in the first place.

It means you can't identify with them because you know no more about what they are like inside than you do about an immobile statue in a park. Lack of communication prevents both parties from interactively adjusting their thoughts and behavior to each other, because you can't adjust to someone if you don't understand anything about them in the first place. Failure to adjust equals failure to communicate equals emotional unavailability.

Even when the norm is ongoing communication, should something reduce or scale down communication, as with a man who does not want to deal with his companion after a stressful day at work, short-term emotional availability decreases in direct proportion to the reduction of truthful open communication. Emotional availability comes down to a man's availability for expressing his true personality and feelings as one way of meeting his partner's need to perceive and experience his true self.

As communication and identification decrease, the taking-on of role behavior appropriate for intimacy decreases and emotional availability withers on the vine. Emotional availability blooms only in proportion to the degree to which adult communication between two people is the norm. As communication dries up, so does emotional availability, and the cold night of the heart closes in.

Chapter Six
Male And Female
Emotional Socialization

Women Get Early Practice
At Taking On Multiple Roles

Women have a greater propensity to become emotionally available than men. Women are pushed from their early years on by peers, role models and their instinctual drives to take on multiple roles. Even little girls like dolls, which allow them to act out their nascent maternal instincts and try on for size a childish version of the mother role they experience with their own mothers.

Mothers reinforce this push for their daughters to take on varied roles by chiding their daughters from late childhood on to dress certain "lady-like" ways, which at that age means simulating some aspects of the social role of lady, a particular social role women evolved primarily for interactions with men. Women also practice taking on certain roles when with their girlfriends, mutually reinforcing each other's social and biological tendencies.

The end result of such female-on-female socialization is that, starting early in life, women get encouragement from several directions to take on varied roles for different social audiences, laying the groundwork for the communicative facility and identification with others that leads to emotional availability. By contrast, few boys get any practice at varied role simulations, such as playing with baby dolls, to encourage them to develop their paternal tendencies.

Natural tendencies plus early practice thus give women a head start at taking on multiple roles to develop the social competencies that underlie emotional availability. Women might wonder why men have a problem in this regard.

The answer is that men stay busy as boys learning the prerequisites of acquiring status, a means of attracting women when they are grown, and are not preoccupied with what to do, say and think once in contact with grown women. Competition is the male road to acquiring status. Boys play games involving male-on-male competition and aggression, the developmental form of the competitive games they later act out in schools and the workplace. Competition and aggression are related to dominance.

The two sexes take different routes at different speeds to reach their respective sexes' definitions of maturity. Men as a group are statistically less likely than women to develop into emotionally complete adults because fewer influences in their upbringing and socialization push them in that direction than is the case among women. Status requires taking on multiple social roles and developing communicative and social adaptation skills that eventually result in most boys acquiring some emotional availability capacities on the side, though not by intent.

The roles young boys take on tend to be roles acted out for other males, involving women or girls only on the periphery, if at all. Not all members of both sexes make it all the way. The road of life is populated with dropouts from the race to develop emotional availability. Dropouts are much more common among the male sex because men receive less developmental encouragement than women to develop these capacities, and this is often due to paternal influences.

Role Model Problems

Boys and girls learn to take on certain roles by watching the most accessible of role models: their mothers and fathers. In an ideal world, boys and girls would have parents in emotionally functional relationships to use as templates for rough approximations of adult behavior, relationships and some of the more visible outward aspects of emotional availability. Children should grow up with some familiarity with those roles implanted in their minds by virtue of observation and slowly growing into fulfilling similar roles themselves.

The problem with this rosy picture is that few parents are perfect, and many have problems even being adequate. Many parents have problems they pass along to their children, either by acting as role models for problem behavior or by directly instructing children in socially inappropriate behavior. Divorce provides a case in point. Over half of all marriages wind up in divorce court. The children of divorcees often develop predictable traits, one such trait being the unfounded suspicion that they in some way bear responsibility for their parents' divorce. Boys who live with divorced mothers with no full-time adult male role models anywhere in sight fill in the blanks about how they suppose adult male role models behave in a predictable manner. Even fathers who are present may not be helpful.

They use information garnered from the entertainment medium of television and peer groups of similarly uninformed and misinformed boys. The behavioral outcome is that such boys learn early in life to look to their peer groups, not adults, for behavioral cues. The answers peer groups provide typically involve using adolescent frames of reference to address adult problem situations. The more absent from the scene one or more parents, the greater the grip peers and television get on the minds of boys by default. The whims of the peer group become their primary guide and television fills in many of the remaining blanks.

Emotional availability remains fixated on the adolescent level on which the peer group expects members to keep it so long as members continue deferring to their peer groups. Boys who look to other boys for answers to adult concerns are driving on a dead-end street. None of them have undergone the sort of maturational experiences they need to become emotionally adult males, and they thus have nothing of value to impart to each other. Their mutual behavioral expectations keep all frozen on the same low level of social-emotional development. Peer group pressures and child-of-divorce roles are two examples of roles that can develop deep roots in the personality early in life and later inhibit the eventual development of emotional availability.

Alcoholic parents have similarly depressing effects on emotional availability. Even should a boy never touch a drop himself, growing around unpredictable, drunken, erratic and possibly violent parents tilts them away from emotional availability. If you don't know how your mother or father will react from one day to the next, you develop the bedrock notion that people in general can't be trusted.

You develop personality characteristics rooted in that fundamental premise that it does no good to open yourself up to people, because they have radically different personalities from one day to the next. You generalize from your experiences and develop a composite picture of what you think the world is like. Such children often grow up to be unspontaneous, emotionally stunted, noncommittal, perfectionistic adults.

The offspring-of-an-alcoholic role is actually a single social role children learn to take on as a byproduct of adapting to formative experiences with a social audience of one or more alcoholic parents. This role blocks them from learning to take on other social roles should the behavioral expectations of those roles conflict with that role's behavioral expectations. Boys from homes where emotional inhibition and unpredictable behavior are the norm will carry that image of the world into other relationships in adult life.

They often get few opportunities to be around other types of people and develop more emotionally expressive ways of dealing with others, because being around alcoholic parents warps the development of their interaction skills starting early in life. Some people shy away from them, sensing their lack of certain social capacities. Such people have no personal experience at expressing themselves in fully adult ways. They develop emotional blank spots in their personalities, where others have lives where those blanks are colored in by, and filled out by, emotionally expressive experiences.

Living this role can prevent them from taking on adult roles, such committing to a steady career or another person. Decades of practice at taking on this role wears a groove in their minds that reinforces their subconscious ties to their upbringings. They get no practice at other roles, so this role fills out by default to encompass the other parts of their lives. Such people can change. Change requires recognizing that being like this is a self-limiting role that served a need when they had no choice about contact with alcoholic parents, but remains a role they must outgrow to become emotional adults. They can cast off this role by practicing taking on other adult roles that allow them to more fully express their emotional and experiential potential and learn how to better relate to others.

Women And Roles

Women evolved in the Stone Age to fulfill roles in all-female cooperative social groups that were probably more closely knit than male hunting groups. Gathering fruits and vegetables is a slow, socially cooperative enterprise allowing for more verbal interaction that is the case for groups of men who quietly tracked and hunted fresh meat. Stone Age women probably had to attract mates if they wanted to fully provide for their offspring, given the extent to which the burdens of Stone Age childrearing slowed down their food-gathering activities. Women back then knew that their long term reproductive prospects were aided by playing a role that met male expectations for women. Having a mate who brought home food was a great survival aid back in the Stone Age.

Women take on roles tailored to local definitions of what men find attractive, because local definitions tell them what is the best possible form of adaptation to local social environments filled with men. The female capacities for speech and taking on roles are tied in some way to enhancing their reproductive interests in the context of living in small tribes of hunter-gatherers. Speech is closely tied to our ability to take on roles, and serves another key function. Women probably evolved greater verbal capacities than men in part also because it was in our species' survival interests to have verbally proficient women raise and socialize children while men were on extended treks to the prairies and jungles hunting meat animals.

The consuming female interest in appearance and fashion, around which entire industries have sprung up, are actually means for enhancing a woman's prospects for initially attracting a high-status male. What women are really buying are mate attraction accessories that help women present themselves in the most favorable visual terms when they take on roles for interaction with men. Evidence of this can be seen throughout history in women's fashions. Bizarre hats, unusual forms of jewelry, dresses ranging from miniskirts to corseted hop skirts – all are female adaptations to social environments filled with differing sorts of men, though some fashions are more due to female introspection or fantasy than actual male interests.

By contrast, male fashions are largely functional, and may take decades to change at even a glacial pace, as the example of business suit lapels demonstrates. The roles women take on for men have a strong visual attraction component, whereas the roles men take on for women have a strong social status component requiring women to have a variety of social evaluation skills if they are to understand where men stand in the local social hierarchies. Women socially reinforce in other women what women as a group expect of other representatives of the female sex in their public social roles, including dress. This is less common among men, who generally feel less need to tell other men how to shape up to help men as a group present a united front to women as a group.

The other side of the equation is the male struggle to acquire the local definitions of status symbols, which provide evidence of their ability to provide for the young as well as child-rearing mothers, meaning the male adaptation to a social environment filled with women. Status can excuse many social failings, at least in the minds of those women who are willing to trade off the social skills that tend to produce emotional availability for symbols of status, such as money and possessions. An affluent social illiterate can thus sometimes do better in some local singles markets than a poverty-stricken male social lion, because some heavily instinctual women are attracted to what their instincts say are the survival advantages of social status versus the optional cognitive luxury of emotional availability.

Male-Female Differences And
Emotional Availability

Biologically speaking, men and women only need to interact to mate, and, to a lesser extent, mutually contribute to the care and feeding of their offspring. This is the lowest-common-denominator biological/instinctual level of human interaction, which is furthered by a large measure of instinctual sexual attraction.

Of course, we do not have to settle for this bare-bones version of social interaction. Our lives can be as socially rich and diverse as we are willing to work at making them. We can stick around others a lot longer than the mating season should we see beneficial reasons to do so. The mental pleasure we derive from continuing interaction with each other is one such reason to stick around.

Emotional availability is not instinctual behavior, though it is rooted in our inborn social instincts. We have the capacity to become emotionally available because our minds are versatile enough to stretch in that direction, and a thousand other directions as well. It requires practice and experience at interaction with others to create the experiential foundation of social interaction out of which being emotionally availability derives. Like most learned skills, the more you do it, the better you get at it. The implication is that while instinctual sexual and romantic attraction might initially bring two people together, the desire for continued and deepened contact with each other requires adjustment to, learning about, and enjoying interaction with, each other. Adjustment requires various forms or verbal and nonverbal communication – talking, touching, gesturing and the like - with each other.

Men and women sometimes do not find it easy to adjust to communicating with each other, or sometimes even want to communicate with each other. Men and women are different. The inborn wiring of their brains makes them perceive some parts of life in fundamentally different ways, which sets different priorities on what is considered important by each sex. Most people will acknowledge that men evolved to be hunters who enjoy the company of other male hunters simply because they think alike and communicate about matters of common survival interest most readily with those with whom they share similar forms of neural wiring. Men share a lot of understandings and inclinations simply by virtue of being men.

Women similarly find it easier to talk with other women, whose brains and bodies evolved around the fruit and vegetable gathering functions their evolutionary ancestors performed and the species-survival functions of reproduction and child-rearing. Maintaining a relationship beyond initial attraction thus requires learning about social interaction and adjusting ourselves based on what we learn about others. This requires communicative experiences with the other sex as a prerequisite for identifying with them, understanding them, adjusting to them and entering into adult relationships with them.

People who fail to identify with, understand and adjust to others are usually predestined for a lifetime of short-term relationships. Their lack of these capacities offers other adults little of interest beyond novelty and sexual attraction. Emotionally available adults do not seek out emotionally unavailable non-adults for long-term relationships. Emotional availability is thus dependent on both acquiring information about others and developing social skills specific to communicating with the other sex.

These are simply preconditions, not guarantees of either a relationship or emotional availability. Situational factors and personality quirks can still make an emotionally unavailable object out of someone who, at least on paper, ought to be emotionally available. The interpersonal dynamics of two people hold the key to the door of emotional availability, but learned social skills allow one opportunities to turn the key and open the door once you find a person whose door is open to your approach and the keys you present.

Role Audiences

We put on role performances to impact audiences in the sense of producing changes in audience thought and behavior to benefit ourselves. Performing for a particular type of social audience can become both addictive and limiting, as any addiction can be. Some actors get used to being in the limelight and being applauded. You can get a bit too used to doing certain things and getting a guaranteed payoff in return, while tuning out other audiences, roles and payoffs. Should men become addicted to performing for male peer-group audiences early in life, that will often become their primary social reference audience, as with a man socialized to act in certain generalized ways by his role as a member of a street gang.

The problem this situation presents is that the primary audience of such men is other men. Women become, not the audience for another sort of primary relationship or different audience for another sort of role, but rather part of the stage on which the man puts on his performances for his primary social audience, meaning other men.

Women are often unaware this, but their disbelief or lack of knowledge does not alter the reality of the situation. Some peer-oriented men consider women to be stage props that offer relief from sexual tensions while the men carry on with role performances for an unseen audience of male peer spectators. Some peer-oriented women similarly consider nothing private in describing their intimate encounters to other women.

The less spontaneous and less emotionally available the man, the more rigidly scripted and rehearsed his "lines" will be, and the more likely it is that, although alone with a woman, he is acting out a role for an imaginary male peer group audience that he carries around in his head with him. He just can not get his male peer group, and what they think of him and expect of him, out of his head. More importantly, he cannot identify with women and see things as they do. When a man cannot identify with women, he has no choice but to fall back on "lines" when dealing with them. He does not understand them well enough to fine-tune his conversations with them. The most that women can expect from such men is for the man to seek sexual applause for an inauthentic imitation of authentic emotion. Men who use elaborate scripted roles picked up from other men to interact with women are emotionally hollow shells who can't be trusted regardless of what they claim to feel. Everything they do is an act, and has no more emotional substance than any other work of fiction.

Male And Female Role Audiences

Men and women think, act and dress differently when with the other sex than with members of their own respective sexes. Each sex relaxes more in certain ways with psychologically adult members of their own sex as compared with the other sex, in the sense of feeling freer to talk about their presentations for the other sex, and allowing for mutual examination and commentaries on their role presentations and the exchange of ideas. While a husband and wife can let down their hair with each other about how they feel about the bosses they have to perform for on the job, they still keep a few things to themselves about what they think of each other. Many things that they do not feel free to say to each other eventually do find ears with a same-sex audience.

The roles each sex takes on when with members of their own sex differs substantially for each sex. Each sex has brains neurally wired for somewhat different styles of communication. Men are almost always more reserved when with an audience of other men than are women when with an audience of other women. The male of our species is more physically aggressive than the female of our species. Even their rest-and-recreation periods have an undercurrent of competition and aggression. Sports, for example, are simply ritualized forms of combat intended to allow for the venting of aggressive impulses without doing permanent damage to participants. Also keep in mind that a large part of male competition comes down to competition for the local definition of status symbols as a means of attracting female companions. In one society it might be money, in another it might be fishing hauls or the ability to hunt whales. Whatever the society, the women are always closely attuned to whatever the local definition of status might be, as well as which men have it and which men do not.

Men generally do not bare their hearts and souls to other men, even their best friends, to the degree to which women routinely do so with other women. This has implications for emotional availability. Women need to know that not only is emotional availability a learned or acquired trait, but also that it is a trait that men are very unlikely to learn from being with other men.

Few male social groups encourage this. Men are not expected to take on emotionally available roles with other men, do not have male role models for emotional availability (boys are rarely, if ever, within earshot when their parents have intimate conversations) and generally get little, if any, practice with other men in taking on a spontaneous, individualistic emotionally available role.

Male-on-male relationships are not a psychological greenhouse suitable for raising the hothouse orchid of emotional availability. They are rather a desert peopled with clusters of superficially affable, rigid cactus plants that seem nice enough but which will often stick you with their needles should you move in too fast and try to get too close. Most men have had a few bad experiences early in life at being taken advantage of by other men, which leads many to keep their guard up most of the time. They carry this habit over to their dealings with women. Men are indoctrinated from early in life, either by example or unconscious social osmosis, to be outwardly reserved in showing their feelings to other men, conduct that becomes so ingrained that it can kicks in even when they are drunk.

They know that emotional behavior might often get them labeled as "wimps" other men, including fathers, feel free to kick around verbally, physically or both. Men think that whatever they say and do might be used against them sooner or later, and often they are correct. By contrast, most women get some experience at taking on modified emotionally expressive roles with other women.

Women are usually not looked down on for crying on another woman's shoulder, asking for advice about relationships and the like. Women have different role expectations for each other when no men are around, and their expectations allow more latitude for emotional expression and emotional availability than is the case for the role behavior expectations men have for other men.

Men and women are each other's audiences, and proper role-taking with the other sex requires varied forms of adjustments in our speech and thinking specific to relationships with the other sex. We all must take on social roles to get through life, and the role we take on with the other sex is one such role. We simply cannot act with the opposite sex as we do with our own sex, though we can crash our ships of self trying to make the mistaken idea that there are no real differences between the sexes work out. Fruitful interaction between the sexes requires a personal experiential database derived from real-life interactions, and this sort of database is best acquired as early in life as possible through direct interaction with members of the other sex. Anyone who tries to generalize from dealings with their own sex to the other sex is headed for disaster. Playing for an audience requires knowing in the first place how the audience thinks and what they expect of you.

We self-select ourselves into social groups with members of our own sex starting early in life. A look at any grade school shows that boys socialize primarily with other boys, and girls primarily with other girls. There is a reason for this. We naturally gravitate towards those who look like us because we assume that they think like us or are like us in some way. We have an instinct to both identify with, and join, a social group, given that we are social animals, and physical similarities are one basis for clustering together. While there are broad areas of mutual interest, the two sexes are different. They instinctually think about different sorts of things in different sorts of ways.

Boys usually pick trucks as toys, and girls usually pick dolls as toys. Boys' brains usually come with a greater mechanical capacity than girls', and girls are born with a greater capacity for social relationships. Either sex can increase their respective capacities with learning and practice. Learning to perform social roles for audiences of the other sex is no different in being a learned capability. The more practice men and women get at learning about, and dealing with, the other sex, the better their chances at getting into, and enjoying, fruitful relationships. All that they need to know who think that what they know about people based on what they have learned from their jobs, their own sexes or wishful thinking is correct are headed for social disasters.

The roles men take on channel their thinking in ways compatible with the role behavior they take on for certain social audiences. Men thus choose male workplace companions, drinking partners and the like on the basis of male-on-male partnership notions. Women do much the same with female companions. The problem with this is that men often carry over the thought processes involved in these sorts of interactions from the way they think with male partners/companions to the way they think they should seek out and interact with female companions. The qualities that make for a superficially good male-male companionship are not necessarily the qualities that make for good male-female intimacy and compatibility. The requirements for these sorts of interactions and relationships are quite different than for same-sex interactions, aside from the sexual and physical components.

Male locker-room and drinking partners and partners typically relate to each other on a superficial level, and get a lot of experience at keeping things superficial. Intimate compatibility requires different qualities than those men typically develop in male-on-male role-playing. The qualities that make for good partnerships make for bad intimate compatibility and self-disclosure. A man who acts this way might treat a woman as a good helpmate, a wife, a mother – but not as someone with whom he is intimate and emotionally compatible. Social partnership is a completely different role for a different sort of audience. Emotional availability and intimate compatibility require slowly learning, through ongoing interactions with the other sex, very different sorts of communicative skills and means of expression.

How Social Audiences Warp Emotional Availability

We take on different social roles to meet the expectations of different social audiences. Not very surprisingly, should the central tendency of those audiences tend towards indifference, or even hostility, to spontaneous emotional expression and self-disclosure, individuals who get a lot of practice at playing roles for those audiences tend to become inhibited, repressed and emotionally unexpressive. Should you get a lot of practice at filling a particular role, you grow into that role. You become more comfortable playing that role and fill in the blanks of the other parts of your life with what you infer about the expectations for that role. You eventually grow into that role and become the role by dint of endless repetition. You become the prisoner of the role expectations of others, unless you have a polycentric array of roles and a core personality of individuality with which to balance your life. This includes the roles boys act out for their fathers.

Should a man's primary social audience be one of emotional adolescents, as in an athletic team or fraternity, the nature of the audience determines the limited, or even nonexistent, extent of his emotional availability. You can not expect a man, especially in his most impressionable years, to not take on a lot of the expectations of those for whom he plays roles to obtain social approval and social status. The audience for one role can determine the emotional limits of your other roles, including emotional availability, particularly when that one role is the center of your self-definition.

Emotionally Unavailable Women

Women can be just as emotionally unavailable as men, and just as unsuitable for long term relationships. Emotional availability is a learned or acquired trait, and women are just as capable or not picking up and developing the social skills that derive from taking on, and filling out, multiple social roles for diverse social audiences. Being emotionally available presupposes social and communicative skills acquired from dealings with the other sex as well as a foundation of a sense of security derived from taking on multiple social roles. Women thus can suffer the effects of these deficits just as much as men.

Women can develop personalities, and deficient social skills, just as warped as men by focusing their lives around one social role, such as their job, They will fail to develop a multiplicity of social interaction skills, particularly those related to female-male relationships and communication. A woman with little experience in getting close to with men will probably try to speak with and relate to them as she does with her girlfriends, a guaranteed social disaster. Emotionally unavailable women are thus often so because they are finely-adjusted to a social environment of other women, and have failed to adjust to social environments full of men.

There are sex differences. There are probably a smaller number of female social isolates than male social isolates. Women define themselves more in terms of their social relationships then do men, probably due to some genetically-determined instinctual imperative that forces women to seek to tie into social networks and relationships to a greater degree than is the case for men. This makes survival sense in terms of our Stone Age evolution, because women who had the social skills to attract and retain mates who would bring them extra food had better chances of survival when with children than women lacking those social skills.

Women almost always develop some sort of network of contacts with other women, even if it is only female social isolates contacting other female social isolates. By contrast, a small but real percentage of men feel that social contacts are strictly optional. Men just do not feel the overwhelming biological imperative women do to tie into social support networks. The stereotype of a lone inventor tinkering away in his basement is a male stereotype, not one that usually comes to mind with respect to women.

Women can be alcoholic, domineering, violent and the like, any and all of which prevent them from learning, and taking on, multiple social roles and learning the variegated mix of social interaction skills that are a prerequisite for emotionally available, long-term relationships. Probably the most common sort of emotionally unavailable women are the millions of women scarred by bad relationships. Whatever the cause of their bad relationships, the outcome is that emotionally available men do not see kindred souls in emotionally unavailable women, and few are inclined to try crack through their emotional turtle shells.

Emotionally available men see little of interest in emotionally unavailable women. They pass over seemingly emotionally unavailable women in favor of women who appear to be emotionally available. Emotionally toughened women work hard at preparing to meet men just like the ones who did them wrong, rather than working at meeting totally different types of men. They remain adapted for the past, not for changing themselves to seek a different sort of future.

Why Women Seek Out
Emotionally Unavailable Men

Birds of a feather flock together. Some women seek out emotionally unavailable men because the women themselves are emotionally unavailable. Such emotionally unavailable women can sniff out men like themselves and go on to have one emotionally distant relationship after another. Nothing in their self-selected social environments pushes them in any other direction. They get into a rut and get more and more cumulative practice with each passing year at staying in that rut.

Emotionally unavailable women are often unaware that male personalities become fixed by age thirty or so. They assume that, because women are a bit more adept than men at adjusting to varied social situations, that men will "change" their basic personalities simply because women want them to change. It won't happen. Men take decades to develop their adult personalities in response to experiences with jobs, male companions, good and bad social experiences and the like. After a certain age, they just have too much practice being what they are to change. Women can not turn a bookworm into a social climber, a couch potato into an athlete or an emotional icebox into an emotional fireplace.

They have already been molded into what they are, and the fires that molded them are no longer burning. Women who can't accept men as they are, meaning as off-the-shelf products who are not going to change reveal their own continuing inability to understand men in general, and unwillingness to seek out more compatible types of men. Emotionally unavailable women need to get out more, develop more social skills and learn more about men if they want to become different kinds of women better able to meet different types of men.

Some women think emotionally unavailable men are "exciting." They see such men as challenges to their feminine capacities. They think that they can find some way to "bring them out." This almost never works. Emotionally distant men have a lot of cumulative practice at remaining emotionally unavailable. They will probably stay that way. Some might change, but such men must start acquiring, possibly decades after they should have started doing so, the social, communicative and expressive skills they did not acquire early on. Do you want to be their teacher? And, more to the point, do you want to be the tutor they wave goodbye to as they move on to greener pastures?

As men become more emotionally available, they see finer distinctions both in themselves and in women they never noticed before. You might no longer be what they want relative to the new personalities they develop as they become more mature and emotionally available. You can't expect men to change in ways guaranteed to benefit you personally, so don't invest years of your life in ploughing a fallow field.

Social pressures from other women can be a woman's emotional downfall. While other women are guaranteed to quietly pressure women in general to get involved with men, the sort of lowest-common denominator men that groups of women "approve" of are not necessarily the sort of men that might be in a particular woman's personal best interests. There is nothing wrong with a man having money, money being a sign of his ability to take on a self-supporting social role in a workplace. But focusing on money as the only trait of interest in a man shows a lack of understanding about men as well a total lack of understanding about what is involved with waking up with a man every day.

While every woman has to decide on what she wants in her basket of desirable qualities in man, women who settle for emotionally unavailable men will probably always feel that something important is missing from their lives. Such women will find out the precise value of catering to their girlfriends' opinions when they have to wake up with the results of catering to their opinions each morning. Women who let others think for them can expect nothing else.

Chapter Seven
How Men Become Emotionally Available Or Unavailable

Roles Cast A Spell Over Emotional Availability

Roles cast a spell over emotional availability. The particular details of the role, or roles, chosen can enchant the individual either towards or away from developing an emotionally available personality. Casting a spell is the most appropriate of analogies, because, the particular details of a major role can bring you either under the darkest of emotional dark stars or under the brightest of emotional summer daystars. The spell a role casts over your personality can even decide whether your future becomes an open or closed book of emotions. It's not magic, however, but just a matter of the subconscious mind filling in the blanks with whatever it infers seem to fit best with the other details of a given role.

For example, boys grow up learning to not show their feelings and to deal with bad experiences "like a man," meaning not showing how much bad experiences shake them. A decade or two of practicing such behavior among male peers will definitely slow a man down when the notion first comes to mind that he might want to express his feelings with a woman and relate to her on a level beyond the purely sexual. He wonders when he talks with her: will she react to me showing me feelings the same way boys do? Some women do, some don't. By contrast, women grow up with a lot more acceptance and flexibility about expressing feelings to both boys and girls, though much more so with girls. The behavioral legacy imprint of the roles taken on over the years casts a long shadow over a man's potential for emotional availability.

How Role Pressures Affect Emotional Availability

Roles shape male personalities by virtue of reinforcing behavior and thought patterns that are part and parcel of those roles. Conversely, thought and behavior patterns not taken on because they are not within the behavioral dictates of certain roles are less likely to be incorporated into an individual's character structure because such traits are not specifically encouraged. Much of a man's personality is thus likely to consist of traits picked up from the roles taken on and practiced each day. Men become the roles they practice, and their personalities expand or contract to fit the roles taken on. Endless repetition and practice of any sort of trait makes that trait more likely to become embedded in the individual's character structure by dint of sheer practice.

Taking on roles for social audiences of one or more people requires adjusting and tailoring our behavior to suit some sort of real or imagined behavioral expectations of the role's social audience. We talk, dress and even think the way others expect us to because we want to receive the payoffs that other give us for conforming to their expectations. Taking on a role thus means attempting to figure out what one or more other people expect of us and doing what they expect in order to receive some sort of benefits, such as a paycheck, the congratulations of a social group for playing the role, country club membership or some other benefit, physical or psychological. We must cooperate with others to get through life, so it is not surprising that we are equipped to enjoy doing what is essential to our survival, meaning obtaining positive estimations of ourselves from others.

There is a fine line between outward conformity and letting social audiences determine what the individual "should" think and do. The problem is that, in growing into any sort of long-term role, you gradually modify not only your external, physical behavior but also your internal thought processes and attitudes imperceptibly edge towards the end of conformity and more complete integration into "living" a role.

For example, even should you hate your job, just having to act out the role of worker on that job eight hours a day, half of your waking hours, slowly but surely integrates an increasingly larger percentage of your personality around the expectations of that role. Even going through the motions leaves some sort of a watermark on your mind. Should financial necessity require you to work nights and sleep days, you eventually you get used to sleeping days and start thinking of yourself as a night owl type, even if you don't care much for being a night owl.

Eating and paying the rent requires doing certain things for social audiences. In those public social roles, the audiences decide what you "should" and should not think and do. Once you are off the stage for that role, what you do and think is up to you. Even the best actors and actresses need to go off-stage, take off their role costumes, relax, and express their true personalities. Men lacking core personalities have motivational and personality vacuums into which the expectations of others will flood, take up residence and set down roots. Such men are not emotionally available. Mechanically acting out others' social expectations without critical examination precludes emotional availability. Emotional availability is a private matter, not a matter for public scrutiny or commentary. It is tied to what the individual wants for himself in an intimate companion, not what others think he ought to want. Acting out roles can help a man develop a repertoire of social skills useful in communicating emotions. This must be mediated by a strong sense of individualistic autonomy so a man can decide just who he wants to get involved with in the first place.

Emotional Availability Is An Acquired Trait

Men are not born emotionally available. They learn to become emotionally available, or unavailable, through a slow process of socialization. They learn what others expect of them and acclimatize themselves to playing a variety of social roles with attendant responsibilities. Two particular types of social roles are particularly relevant to the development of emotional availability.

One is the public role men take on – if they take on any role at all – for women in general. Role here means their general attitude towards women – respect or contempt. That role is itself influenced or determined by some primary role, or roles, they take on, such as their workplace role and how they treat women in the workplace or the role-related attitudes towards women they acquire in their male peer groups.

The second role of interest is the role taken on in their one-on-one intimate relationships. This might be influenced by some other primary role, as with a man psychologically dependent on his mother who models his behavior with other women on his relationship with his mother. Emotional availability partially develops out of, and derives from, previous relationships, mass media, and contacts with peers, parents and role models. Men learn – or refuse to learn – how to become emotionally available. Men must necessarily take on the responsibilities of at least one major life role, and several minor satellite roles, and not all of those roles encompass expectations that men become emotionally available with women.

Should men not practice becoming emotionally available, they get there less often than men who do practice being emotionally available. As men have unstructured contacts with women, they develop inferred understandings about women based on those contacts, learn to identify with women and gradually come to disclose and express themselves with the right kinds of women and eventually male themselves emotionally available with compatible women.

Some men become quite experienced at staying emotionally unavailable. A pimp is an extreme example. Regardless of how he positions himself to the public and with his private coterie of subjects, he is not emotionally available. No man who fills that role, wherein he sells the sexual services provided by women he coerces, can be emotionally available. They are two-legged predators with well-polished, and often violent, manipulative reactions designed to control their victims. Their role behavior extends into every crevice of a pimp's life, and taints all of their contacts with women.

They have no interest in what women feel or think, and even less interest in adjusting their own thoughts and behavior to equal relationships with women. All of their behavior and attitudes towards women derives from their pimp role, and they have years of ingrained experiences at being what they are. They do not just shift gears and take on another role when they get off from "work." A wolf does not stop being a wolf at five o'clock. Emotional availability never develops in such men. Supposed exceptions are simply polished liars out to con someone or everyone. No woman with any intelligence would see anything to gain from associating with such men, who get huge amounts of practice at using, manipulating and mistreating woman. Their lives offer women nothing on which to build a relationship.

Women who come into contact with emotionally unavailable men similarly adjust their own personalities to dealing with such men on a daily basis. Consider the extreme example of a prostitute. Most of her relationships with men are with pimps and customers for their sexual services. Taking on this role reinforces the attitudes towards men encouraged by this role. They carry over the attitudes their roles encourage to their after-hours lives. Their work role specifically discourages the development of emotional availability and intimate communications with "customers," and reinforces the general idea of associating men and sex with money.

Not surprisingly, many prostitutes become sexually frigid and have troubles with orgasms. Nothing in their roles encourage spontaneity or intimacy, so it does not develop. They get no practice being with men who can elicit self-disclosure from them, and become unlikely to develop in that direction because such men as they usually come into contact with do not encourage them to develop such traits. Their customers bring nothing to their "relationships" but money.

Individuality And Emotional Availability

Expressing individuality enhances the search for compatible others. A free flow of information about yourself helps others determine the prospects for interpersonal compatibility, enhancing your chances of having enjoyable experiences by increasing your chances of meeting someone compatible. As you express your individuality and disclose yourself to others, you improve your chances of making contact with others who like what you express about yourself.

Men and women who don't express and disclose what they reduce their chances of meeting someone compatible. Nobody can figure out whether or not they are compatible because they know nothing about them in the first place. You can't evaluate compatibility if you don't know anything about them in the first place.

Emotions are individualized communications about your feelings and thoughts. They necessarily derive from a combination of your individual experiences and your similarly individualized inclinations, capacities and preferences. Mimicking someone else's forms of emotional expression won't work. Emotional forms of expression arising out of another person's experiences and personality will never fit properly on someone else. You must express your own emotions in your own way, not mimic the emotions of others.

Mimicking what you see actors and actresses doing in a movie blocks you from developing your own unique forms of emotional expression and denotes a lack of individuality. Emotional availability is a similarly individualistic matter of expressing your deeper emotions and preferences to someone of your choice. Both the emotions expressed and your choice of companions with whom you make yourself emotionally available are individualized choices.

Emotional Availability And Status

Social status promotes a man's potential for becoming emotionally available, but does not guarantee it in and of itself. It is not social status per se that is tied to emotional availability, but rather an internal biological/psychological process triggered by social status.

Social status is a locally-defined matter. Status in an Eskimo community differs substantially from status in a complex urbanized technological society, because the survival requirements differ in those societies. Whale blubber is crucial in Eskimo communities, so whale-hunting ability confers status on men with that ability. Money is the technological society's analog of whale blubber. It aids survival in our society, so men pursue it. Acquiring it confers status, and men feel better about themselves because they have status, and women like men sporting the local definition of social status.

Some aspects of social status are constant across societies. Human beings are biologically hardwired to be both sensitive to, and responsive to, the social reactions of others to how they are perceived, and to react to the activities and opinions that determine social status. Our minds are specifically geared to react to how others evaluate us. Others perceive us, and evaluate us, by means of what we communicate about ourselves using words, facial expressions, body postures and symbolic means such as letters and e-mail. They can express how they evaluate of us using these same mediums of communication. Whatever medium others people use to communicate their opinions and assessments of us, we are biologically hardwired to take note of them and react to them.

Hormones such as serotonin flow into our bodies when we perceive others assessing us positively. Our perception that we have social status increases the flow of serotonin into our bodies. Serotonin produces a state of mental calm and satisfaction with life, and simultaneously dampens aggressive impulses. Artificial serotonin is often used to treat depression, because it improves the users' outlook on life by altering their internal perception of having social status, thereby lessening their potential for aggression and improving their capabilities for peaceful social interaction. The purely psychological effects of hormones such as serotonin provide biological proof that we are social animals. Our evolution of this hormonal capacity shows that we are geared for both social interaction and to feel enjoyment in social interaction.

Hormones play a role in confirming social status, and also play a role in emotional availability. Such hormones relax men to the extent that they calm down enough to open up emotionally, disclose themselves to others and engage in open and relaxed relationships. Men lacking serotonin to calm the mind and body feel on edge. They overflow with anxiety (or depression) about their lack of social status, and have problems handling fully functional adult relationships.

This reaction to the lack of status may have evolved as nature's way of ensuring that only men who already have the survival advantages that come with the local definition of social status (such as money or whale-hunting ability) are relaxed enough to get into relationships. Being in adult relationships requires being calm enough to engage in relaxed social discourse with females and not see self-disclosure as a psychological threat. Only those who feel that they have something to hide feel the need to hide what they are from others.

On the other side of the social equation, female interest in male status has evolutionary survival value for children. During most of our evolutionary history, women had limited mobility during pregnancy, and, to a lesser extent, while childrearing. Women were partially dependent on their mates to bring home enough food so that pregnant women could "eat for two." Back then, the men with the most status were probably the men who could hunt and bring home the most food. The man who brought home the most food probably had the most to spare for his mate and children. More hunting ability equaled more status equaled more food equaled more desirable to women. Women thus evolved the capacity to seek out men with high status as an aid to their own, and their offspring's, long-term survival prospects.

Empathy And Role Repertoires

Emotional availability rests on a foundation of identification-derived understanding of, and trust for, selected members of the other sex. A man who distrusts women will not attempt to understand them and will never become emotionally available. He will not express or disclose himself with those he does not trust.

Should he regard members of the other sex simply as sexual trading partners unworthy of long-term commitments and unwelcome in the man's home-base territory, empathy for women will never take root and emotional availability will be derailed before it gets started. The greater the extent to which a man has been socialized in single-sex environments wherein women are seen as interlopers good only for sexual recreation, the less likely he is to take on roles, or role characteristics, that enhance his emotional availability with women. Developing a new mindset conducive to emotional availability is an uphill battle for such men, and some are not inclined to even try. They are comfortable the way they are, surrounded by other men who think as they do and who pressure them to stay the way they are and by force of example.

Empathy for women is most likely to develop in men who take on multiple roles and responsibilities for multiple social audiences of both sexes. Men socialized primarily among other men are less likely to see woman as beings akin to themselves but rather as objects for hunting and snaring, figures of speech few women find endearing.

Empathy will most likely flourish when men have regular informal contact with women and opportunities for unstructured social contact outside of the context of formal public social roles. They need informal unstructured opportunities for interaction if they are to develop their social skills. It is crucial that men have informal social contact with women outside of the scripted social roles.

Informal social contact allows men to learn to identify with women and see women as people, rather than as distant objects of desire to be approached with scripted lines as a hurried preliminary to intercourse. Men who deal with women in a variety of contexts slowly come to think of them from a variety of angles and perspectives, build up a composite mental picture of women and their ways, and use what they collect as a basis for informed conversations and adjustive interactions. They adapt how they think and talk with social audiences of women based on what they learn. As men learn more, some develop empathy, and some do not.

By contrast, one-role men often have one-track minds regarding women. Many one-role men consider women good for "one thing," and only one thing, period. Given that they define themselves in one-note, one-role terms, it should as no surprise that they define women along one dimension as well. A social role and self-definition will pattern and channel a man's thoughts into patterns and configurations defined by the social role.

Since fulfilling a public social role necessarily involves the man doing something others want or expect of him, such as being the boss, he must turn off his own thoughts, feelings and ideas in fulfilling that role. Empathy is not a role requirement for most roles men fulfill, but rather something a man must develop on his own for his own benefit.

Empathy and emotional availability thus are most likely to develop as a thing apart from fulfilling any sort of socially scripted, or job-related, role. They are core personality characteristics, meaning individual choices made by autonomous individuals. Emotional availability is an individual matter of deciding what to be. Practicing social conformity, meaning becoming what groups of others expect of you, is a habit of mind that necessarily blocks the expression of individual-oriented emotional availability.

Do not assume that fulfilling any single role, no matter how prestigious that role, leads to emotional availability and empathy, though fulfilling multiple roles with varied responsibilities for diverse social audiences will definitely expedite its development. One-track minds rarely, if ever, switch to the autonomous track carrying passengers along the road of empathy and emotional availability.

Boys Get Minimal Practice At
Being Emotionally Available

A large proportion of boys grow up with little contact with women beyond the superficial. Even mothers rarely tell boys much about how girls and women think. Most early-life male socialization derives from either male role models or the male peer groups to whose expectations boys gradually learn to look to for behavioral guidance.

Even the mothers of some such boys might upbraid them to "act like a big boy, not a sissy" and so on. Such mothers thus become female surrogates for male-on-male socialization. As a result, many boys get little real experience at taking on roles for female social audiences (beyond the negative role of not doing what mommy tells you to do).

By early adolescence, they have little feel for what girls or women expect of them and how the other sex thinks. Boys remain unable to identify with women because they do not understand them very well in the first place. On those occasions when they do have to act out roles for female audiences, what is requested of boys is most often just more of the same sort of expectations they get from male audiences.

Thus, it should come as no surprise that many men act emotionally unavailable with women because learning to become emotionally available was never required of them as part of any roles they took on as boys. By early adolescence, many boys have little experience at taking on roles for female audiences other than their mothers and teachers.

Women should not wonder why many young men have bad manners with women. They spent most of their formative years with male audiences, and developed ingrained habits from years of practice at being around all-male audiences. If boys never really catch on to the idea that women are a social audience for whom they need to learn to understand and adjust their behavior, it should come as no surprise that they wind up not adjusting their thoughts and behavior to women, and are slow to develop self-disclosure and emotional availability competencies.

Emotional availability is not encouraged by their male peers, and they are not prompted by female peers – those with whom they have contact, anyhow - to become emotionally available. The specific lack of male expectations that boys in male peer groups become emotionally available is thus a major cause of emotionally unavailable behavior and personalities among men. Lack of practice and exposure is the key.

Boys garner social applause from other boys during their formative years before adolescence for exhibiting traits such as aggression and competition. Women are literally a foreign species for many young men before their early teens. Emotional availability is at the end of a long line of adult development and social interaction activities with women. You can hardly expect boys growing up in a male-centered social universe to become emotionally available if the central tendency of their social development has specifically discouraged the development of such traits.

Learning to tune into female expectations, identifying with women and adjusting their thoughts and behavior accordingly tends to come into the personality picture only after the major building blocks of boys' personalities are already in place, and these new expectations often must be adjusted around what is already locked into place in boys' minds. They have too much mental furniture already in place for women to just drop something discordantly oriented towards a new social audience of women and not expect it to get pushed off into a corner where it will not contrast with the pre-existing furniture already in place.

By contrast, girls typically grow up with some sort of experience at taking on childish roles accompanied by dimly-perceived second-hand expectations involving males in roles in the background of their children's play activities. Girls who play with baby dolls usually have some vague idea that mommy and daddy dolls are out there overseeing their own "dolls." The idea that girls will someday take on roles for male audiences is planted early, and girls begin to mentally fill out the roles in their minds starting at an early age.

Even if these make-believe roles are the sheerest of fantasies, the seed of taking on roles for male audiences is planted. Since taking on a role such as wife or "mommy" necessarily involves the social adaptation of one's self to at least some expectations of the male audience, the idea of taking on multiple roles takes root earlier in female minds than in male minds, usually enhancing the prospects for the future development of emotional availability in women. No such seed is planted in boys' minds by engaging in role-playing activities such as cowboys.

A man's capacity to feel and express emotions with a woman will be stunted, or possibly fail to develop beyond the juvenile level, should they not be specifically practiced and developed in real-life social interactions. You don't develop the capacities of your heart and lungs by daydreaming about exercise, and the same applies to emotional capacities that can be developed only in real-life relationships.

Roles For A World They Never Made

Everybody seems to have ideas about what the young ought to be taught, and pressures to adopt roles are pushed on boys starting early in life. Adults want boys to be predictable, and roles are one way to make them more so. The outcome is that everybody, except those under pressure to take on certain types of role behavior, has a say in what the role expectations for the role in question will be. Everyone has to pick from the deck of cards handed to them, and nobody gets to design their own deck of societal cards. We can not create new societies from the ground up so as to give ourselves role choices more to our liking.

Examples of this abound. Let's say you were born in a totalitarian society, and grew up being taught and being expected to follow, the "party line," meaning role expectations about personal characteristics such as conformity and not questioning authority. The role expectations such societies offer you would not encourage you to develop personality traits such as individuality and entrepreneurship, since such values are contrary to the core values of such societies. The role choices offered to the young operate channel and direct the development of certain types of character structures and necessarily include certain types of character traits and exclude others. Every role specifies certain traits and un-specifies others, either directly or by implication.

The types of roles typically offered to young males rarely, if ever, include any sort of opportunities for the development of emotional availability. This is considered an optional, or even undesirable, trait for development in young boys in many parts of Western societies. Our societal consensus just does not see such traits as worthy of public promotion. It may not actively discourage it, but does not actively promote it either. Some traits are openly encouraged, while others are encouraged only implicitly, or not really discussed at all. A major portion of one's personality is thus often largely socially determined.

Our society's definition of adult includes large measures of psychological autonomy and financial independence from one's parents, but our local definition is not the universal definition. Some societies consider various forms of dependence on one's parents to be a desirable trait, as happens in societies where extended families comprising several generations live under one roof.

Most of the role models and developmental experiences to which boys are exposed encourage traits that match up with adult roles and role characteristics contrary to emotional availability – competition, aggressiveness, conformity as a means of advancement, and so on. Boys are thus primarily socialized to fit into all-male environments, and only incidentally for two-sex environments, except in the most superficial sexual sense. You rarely see or hear about any sort of emotional availability development, because it is an individual, not a group or societal, concern. Men have to pretty much develop it on their own, and many never do, never being encouraged to do so before adulthood. Old habits and social conditioning can die hard.

Social Principles

Some social principles operate to make men emotionally available, some do not. It really depends on just what the specific principles are and what sort of bearing it has on their individual security and autonomy as regards emotional availability. Regardless of how men acquire these particular principles, the net effect is that those principles are consciously and unconsciously applied to a variety of evolving social situations, just as the principles of geometry are applied to an endless variety of geometry problems. Christian and Buddhist societies differ in part because of the different principles instilled in their adherents early in life and applied to personal and societal situations. Some principles discourage emotional availability, while others encourage it, or at least do not actively discourage it.

Growing up in certain types of rigidly-defined family structures, such as the peasant cultures of Southern Europe, where fathers are considered absolute masters always to be obeyed, provides role models and expectations unlikely to be conducive to the development of emotional availability. Domination prevents women in such cultures from expressing a full range of emotions.

In such cultures, emotional availability might even be actively discouraged by society and men in general, because it has the potential to dilute authority and set up unwanted counterexamples of "disrespect" suitable for punishment. Men in such societies are taught that the demands of public social roles always take priority over private social roles and individual needs.

Control-oriented cultures tend be highly instinctual, meaning that instincts such as domination and control prevent the development of the rational communicative capacities that foster the development of emotional availability. Where there is no opportunity for in-depth interaction, top-down communication that imparts a demand for obedience takes priority over everything else. In general, the more control-oriented a society's social principles, the less such societies encourage emotional availability.

Other types of cultural and religious principles, such as charity and forgiveness, probably add to the probability of a man developing emotional availability. It's the particular social principles that matter.

How Groups Reinforce Role Behavior

Groups control the emotional availability of members by enforcing ground rules for limits on freedom of individual expression of emotions as well as choices of potential emotional companions. Social classes, for example, discourage women from entering into serious relationships with men from the social classes lower than their own. Adolescent-minded males of all ages, meaning street gangs, fraternity members, athletic teams, drinking clubs and the like, encourage members to avoid becoming emotionally involved with women and developing serious relationships that detract from their loyalty to the group. They do so because group conformity focuses on the retention of shared characteristics among group members.

Conformity is enforced by means of social pressures and withdrawal of the privileges of group membership, such as access to fraternity parties or the protection of fellow street gang members. At the finish line of years of social-control programming activities, such men wind up having been reinforced to play certain roles and similarly pressured to avoid taking on contrary roles which detract from, or counteract, the hold their peer-group role has on their personalities.

Emotionally Unavailable Types Of Men

There are several types of emotionally unavailable men, and initially profiling two easily recognizable and seemingly divergent types of emotionally unavailable men illuminates the crucial effect that taking on multiple roles plays in promoting male emotional availability.

A college nerd who stays in his room and studies round the clock, coming out only to eat, go to classes and take exams, plays his narrow single role of academically superior student well, but remains a social illiterate saddled with juvenile emotional reactions and social skills because he avoids taking on other social roles. He avoids dealing with people and learning how to interact with them, thus never developing his social interaction skills. Stress about how others perceive him contributes to locking him into an emotionally unavailable role mold and overall life situation. He remains this way until he goes out and has enough social experiences to reach the social-experience "critical mass" level necessary for both higher-level social skills and, eventually, emotional availability.

The nerd experiences and express emotions, but only on a self-centered, childish sort of level, fantasizing about purely physical relationships centered around gratifying his sexual needs. Emotional starvation does not equal emotional availability, because he does not know how to express anything beyond his own need for gratification. The starving man does not have table manners on his mind. He offers little of interest to others until he learns more about interacting with them. He does not know enough about how to express his emotions with others to function in an adult social context. He needs to learn to understand how women think and go on to adjust his thoughts and behavior to being with a female social audience. His social-emotional skills will remain at the starting gate until he starts interacting with women. A nerd fulfills only one social role that does not suit all occasions. Very few nerds are actually completely social isolated, of course. They socialize with other nerds, which operates to further ingrain and reinforce their personality traits.

At first glance, a socially adept fraternity member might seem to be at the opposite end of the social spectrum from the nerd. The reality is that the nerd and fraternity member have more in common than it might appear at first glance. Both types live to fulfill only one social role. Being a fraternity member equates with group membership. Groups pre-select those most likely to work at fitting in, or conforming, and supporting the ideals of the group mentality, and reinforce these tendencies.

Groups recruit prospects predisposed to adapt themselves to group norms for behavior, and work hard at psychologically programming members with guidelines for actions and attitudes for interacting with non-members, including women. This is why poets are so rare in fraternities and athletes so common. Endless social conditioning keeps dissidents from getting out of line, and probably keeps them from joining many such groups in the first place. Anti-intellectuals recruit more of their own kind, not people opposed to their ideals.

Fraternities are territorial groups that pick and choose members whose initial inclinations are much the same as those already in the group. Territorial means that if you are not a member, you are outside their social territory and are perceived as less important than group members. Territorial behavior is purely instinctual behavior, because it automatically classifies all outside the group as being unworthy of meriting the same sort of attitudes and behavioral responses as group insiders, and for no other reason beyond them being outsiders. Note that this instinctual mindset is devoid of any sort of rational or intellectual content.

Outsiders are bad-by-definition, and suitable candidates for victimization as the mood swings of fraternity members dictate. Insiders are good-by-definition for no other reason beyond being group members.

This is the mentality of a tribe of territorial male Stone Age hunters who happen to live in a modern society, but whose attitudes match those of their ancestors from ages past. Fraternity members are thus locked into a single social role. The role into which they are locked is that of group members for whom being in agreement with other group members – also known as conforming – takes precedent over what outsiders think. Intimacy and emotional availability are not traits fraternities do much to encourage.

Nothing in the fraternity mindset, for that matter, encourages such traits. The more the group programs the individual, the less of an individual personality there remains to make choices free of group propaganda. Fraternities are heavily tilted not so much towards adolescent behavior as towards non-adult, anti-intellectual purely instinctual behavior. The less the extent to which the rational part of the human mind is involved, the more apish male hunting group instincts manifest themselves and become the norm.

Not very surprisingly, living in fraternity housing reinforces group ideals. Fraternity members become socially adept by the social standards of public social discourse. They remain emotionally distant, because focused dedication to some group's ideals and standards of behavior spills over into other areas of life. Dedication to fraternity ideals requires dampening or beating down individuality and emotional expression, emotional expression being a form of expression of individual preferences, not a group consensus. Nonconformists inclined towards spontaneous emotional expression have a tough time in fraternities. The last thing a group wants is divided loyalties, meaning someone whose loyalties are divided between allegiance to himself and what the group expects of him.

Fraternities, street gangs, athletic teams and drinking clubs break down individuals and remake them to suit the ideals of the group consensus on individual thought and behavior. Note that some seemingly different types of groups share elements of physical and mental abuse such as fraternity hazing, gang tattooing, branding, drinking marathons and exhausting physical workouts. These sorts of activities create a bond between members who undergo such common privations.

Nothing in these abusive group activities, their initiation activities or training encourages emotional availability in any way. Group bonds based on abuse are not qualities that add anything to adult male-female relationships. The patterned, stereotypical attitudes and behavior towards women found in many men who engage in such group-oriented activities shows how male-bonding stunts emotional availability.

Emotional availability is an individual capacity and a form of expression of personal preferences, not a group activity on which a man needs to get a consensus to express himself.

Certain lifestyles and activities can block this capacity from developing and even cause it to wither away.

The greater the degree to which a man chooses to integrate himself into a conformist, bonded-male group member role, the greater the degree to which his blind deference to the opinions of his male peers will block him from bonding with women and developing emotional communicative capacities. Emotional availability is at the end of a long line of adult development activities, not the beginning, and men who choose to refuse to develop adult capacities wind up at the finish line of adulthood without them.

Peer Opinions And Social Control

Men programmed early enough in life by their peer groups to look to their peer groups for guidance and direction of their personal lives almost never become emotionally available. They sign up to become the prisoners of the opinions of their peer group's opinions. Should this mentality become implanted early enough in life, it becomes impossible to root out later on.

Some men value the opinions of their peer groups to the extent that they are unwilling to get emotionally involved with women, and even avoid public displays of affection that might disconcert peer group members who see them. They get years, and even decades, of practice at being peer-oriented instead of self-directed.

They miss out on endless opportunities to develop emotional capacities by interacting with women in unstructured social contexts. It becomes difficult to turn back the clock later in life and develop wholly different type of personality traits and capacities for intimacy once your basic personality and outlook on life become set in place around age thirty or so.

Peer-oriented men act as if members of their peer group are always listening and watching. They cater to group expectations because they have been conditioned to think that peer opinions take precedence over private relationships and emotions. If their primary source of self-esteem is peer group approval of their behavior, they will ruminate long and hard before going against the group consensus on acceptable behavior. The only emotions peer groups typically approve of is inauthentic, superficial, stereotyped behavior towards women, meaning whatever keeps male-female relationships on the superficial, wholly sexual level.

Superficial men encourage other men to be similarly superficial themselves. Male peer groups will use any pretext to stop member from having anything that the group as a whole does not have. The socially immature are covertly envious of men who can get into real relationships, though few will admit to this. Emotional tendencies can thus be socially pressured out of existence by emotionally unavailable male audiences envious of emotionally available men.

The fewer possibilities for adult development a peer-oriented role offers, the more involvement and channeling of emotional energies the role requires, and the more parasitical the role becomes. A role that offers nothing of emotional value while blocking someone from taking on other roles that allow for emotional involvement with others is almost always parasitical. It feeds on draining emotional energies that might have been diverted into involvement in other roles. The peer group exerts ongoing social conditioning pressures against emotional behavior that is inconsistent with the role of male peer group member, and these pressures lead to this dead-end, one-role group-is-everything mentality that is all too common among street gangs and other types of peer groups.

Street gangs expect members to live, and even die, for the group, and condition and propagandize their members endlessly towards that aim. They really mean it when they say that group members shouldn't trust anyone outside the gang, and women are definitely outsiders. Fraternities are middle-class gangs. They promote socially acceptable forms of instinctual male-bonding group activity, and foster similar, though less intense, feelings of distrust towards outsiders. A gang has its turf territory, and a fraternity has its frat house territory. The differences between fraternities and street gangs are primarily matters of social class, and both types of groups share a focus on the core values of conformity and living to fulfill a single social role.

The greater the degree to which men live to act out social and behavioral roles only for other men, or the degree to which they live and breathe only one social role for a single primary social audience, is the degree to which they are emotionally unavailable to women. Such men are too closely tuned into what other men expect of them to tune into what women expect of them. They cannot tune out what other men expect of them.

What their peer group thinks is not only more important than what women think, it is even more important than what they think of themselves, because their peer group largely controls what they think of themselves as well as what they think of women. Male conformists just don't speak the language of emotional availability and can't be bothered to learn it.

A primary mental undercurrent in a gang's group activities is that members keep acting as group members even when away from the group. Gang members wear their jackets or other gang attire almost everywhere, and frat members wear a condescending attitude towards nonmembers with their frat jackets wherever they go. The degree to which a group requires such behavior of members is the degree to which they are a nonadult group. Adults must act differently with different types of people in order to get through life. Taking on such a nonadult mindset automatically prevents a man from adjusting his thoughts and behavior to other social audiences – including women.

The greater the degree to which male group bonding is grounded in some sort of instinctual, semi-tribalistic group behavior, the less it offers women as a foundation for an adult relationship. A woman will find nothing to build on in any sort of male group bond based on deindividualization or abuse that she can use to foster an adult male-female relationship.

Chapter Eight
Problems That Block
Emotional Availability

Emotional Desert Lizards

Men who've had bad relationships with the wrong sorts of women often react to their experiences by withdrawing emotionally and becoming emotional desert lizards. If a man gets an overdose of the wrong sorts of women early enough in life, his entire personality warps around building up psychological defenses against anticipated recurrences of his bad experiences. Like a broken leg that mended improperly, their emotional availability stays broken and requires extensive in-relationship rehabilitation for them to emotionally ambulate without limping.

Being an emotional desert lizard is a self-induced victim role that reduces emotional availability. Such men grow tough, emotionally reptilian hides to fill out their self-induced role of permanent victim. Taking on the ongoing role of victim in response to past relationships is a permanently self-limiting role that prevents one from taking on more emotionally available roles while producing little for men who take on this victim role. These men reenact in their minds the sort of bad experiences they had and develop hard-bitten, suspicious, distrustful personalities focused around mental simulations of their bad experiences. They are ever-prepared to refight the wars of the past.

Taking on the ongoing single social role of victim negates their potential for adapting to new social environments filled with different types of women. Their personalities become too specialized for generalized male-female interactions, and they tend to seek out what they perceive as non-threatening relationships only millimeters deep in emotional texture.

While being a desert lizard is an appropriate adaptation for parched emotional landscapes, the reality is that they deliberately seek out emotional desert inhabitants and continuously refine their adaptation to emotionally dry landscapes. They live and breathe their victim roles, seeking out only the desert isles they see scattered about an ocean of fresh water. They need only shed their lizard skins to quench their emotional thirst, but most will not do so.

Sometimes the right sort of women can induce a man to emerge from this role and take on a more completely adult role, sometimes not. It depends on the individual, his emotional flexibility and his willingness to change. Getting such men to change first requires getting them to realize that other types of women out there and that becoming involved requires adapting their thoughts and actions to take a different role if they wish to enjoy the benefits of companionship of other types of women. They just cannot act the same way with all types of women. If they don't change, the types of women they meet will also not change.

Roles And Stress

Human beings are biologically adapted to take on a number of roles. This does not mean, however, that they can take on an unlimited number of roles, an unlimited amount of stress or spend unlimited amounts of time on the roles they take on. Stress is a disruption of our state of mind in reaction to real or imagined pressures. There are physical limits to what we can do. These limits are determined by the biological constraints of the human body and mind. Those who try to exceed these limits are headed for burnout or collapse.

We can take on multiple roles, but are limited by the amount of time in a day. Taking on multiple roles during the day is less stressful than taking on only one role, but somewhere in the ten to twelve hours per day range we reach the physical limits of exhaustion and must take off our cloak of roles and relax. The one-role man or woman who works at their single role for ten hours a day, or more, will be more stressed than the person who takes on multiple roles. Both will feel stress, however.

The less mature, one-role man will show visible symptoms of his stress more often, and be less emotionally available than the multi-role man. The unremitting pressure of a one-role life does not have many pleasant side effects for the individual. Some roles, such as air traffic controller or emergency medical technician, are just inherently more stressful than others, and may not leave a great deal of psychological reserves of adaptation energy in reserve. In such cases, less than eight hours a day of such stresses can leave a person drained and in need of rest and recreation before becoming calm enough to become emotionally available.

Emotional availability is openness to the expression of intimacy and self-disclosure. The side effects of taking on other roles should not block the expression of intimacy, and emotional availability flourishes best when the mind is in a low-stress state. As stress increases, emotional availability decreases proportionately. Emotional availability is a hothouse orchid that requires special attention to flower, and not the arctic emotional climate of unremittingly chilly psychological stress. Should one role fall apart, such as the role of employee, a man might take on another role, such as part-time employee at a lower wage, whose payoffs partially counteract the stress resulting from losing the psychological benefits of the lost job.

The most common form of stress is where the expectations of another role preclude, by definition, the development of emotional availability. Workaholism precludes the development of emotional availability because, by the standards of definition of workaholics, work is the purpose of life and everything and everybody else is subordinated to that role. Workaholics both block off opportunities to learn to take on other roles and also suffer the effects of excessive role-induced stress

Stress reduces emotional availability. It drains our energies, leaving us unwilling and unable to communicate in the relaxed and truthful manner emotional availability requires. When a man exceeds his limits of endurance for stress, he shuts down emotionally and may bristle with hostility in reaction to attempts to get him to open up. Women may beg to differ, but men see importuning women who importune stressed men for emotional availability as, at best, unwelcome annoyances.

Even men who are emotionally available under more relaxed circumstances do this. Stress strips away most of the rational-intellectual layers of thinking, including those involved in the communicative aspects of emotional availability. As stress goes up, only survival-related instincts remain percolating below, and the less emotionally available he is at the end of his stressful day.

A life situation wherein a man takes on only one role, or multiple immature roles, multiplies the stress a man experiences. A single-role man does not have the advantage of multiple psychological steam-release valves that taking on multiple roles allows. As with a man who lives and breathes nothing but his job, a bad day on the job is not counterbalanced by good times with the wife and kids. A thirtyish momma's boy who lives with his mother and is a flunky at work feels more job-induced stress than a thirtyish happily married man feels on the same job. The lack of counterbalancing psychological factors makes the difference.

Being forced into an unwanted role can block a man, at least in the short run, from taking on other roles. This is another way stress can overload a man and block emotional availability. A prisoner confined within four walls, with no opportunities to take on other desirable roles (aside from the unwanted role of colleague-cohort of his fellow prisoners) is an example.

Two people can have differing, non-complementary role expectations for each other. Mismatched couples with different personalities and temperaments generate steam pressure stresses of their own. It is a mistake for mismatched couples to stay together. People with diverging expectations will neither change the underlying personalities that induce them to have such expectations, nor will they change. The truthful spontaneity of communication characteristic of emotional availability is absent from such relationships. Such people are on fundamentally different wavelengths, and have differing, non-complementary role expectations for each other. You might as well try to pair off a male dog with a female cat. The beckoning presence of more compatible and enjoyable potential significant others in greener pastures elsewhere makes their confinement to quarters yet more unbearably stressful.

Brain Damage And Emotional Availability

Brain damage and autism have one common characteristic: physically measurable damage to brain cells reduces, or eliminates, the potential for emotional availability. Simply put, emotional availability is completely dependent on the proper functioning of human brain cells. Abnormalities that derive from genetic defects and accidents shed light on emotional expression problems and elucidates some parallels with single-role men.

Autistic children are born with a defect manifested in the form of brain cells with developmental disorders. Brain cells in the limbic system most likely fail to develop into mature brain cells or get organized into faulty neural networks. Autistic adults fail to develop adult social and cognitive skills because their brains lack the sort of mental wiring that allows them to understand other people and emotions. Autistics rarely develop the ability to express themselves in emotionally adult ways. They are emotionally unavailable because they have blank spots in the brain where emotions are generated. Autistics are thus genetically locked into the single role of being autistic. Men who have been in accidents that result in physical damage to the brain can experience similar problems.

There are some parallels between autistics and emotionally unavailable adults. Single-role men are the social analogs of biological autistics. Their emotional unavailability is rooted in social causes instead of the biological, but the end result is much the same: emotional unavailability due to the inability to change. Autistic men are frozen into emotional immaturity by their genes or other aspects of their biology, whereas emotionally unavailable men are frozen into emotional immaturity by immature role choices. No matter what you try to do, autistics lack the brain cells necessary for adult emotional expression and simply cannot act like complete adults. Nonautistic emotionally unavailable men who missed out on taking on multiple roles never become capable of adult emotional expression. They lack the adult emotional capacities they should have developed as a byproduct of having taken on multiple roles for various social audiences. They were unable to use social experiences they did not have as a basis for identifying with women and slowly learning how to meet the behavioral expectations required for adult relationships with women.

Drug Addicts And Mental Patients

Drugs and biochemically-induced, non-situational mental problems such as bipolar disorder disrupt the biochemical equilibrium of the human brain. One effect is an inability to think and act like an emotionally available adult. The adult capacities of the brain are warped or suspended by these foreign substances until such time as the brain is clear of them. Even then, the long-term presence of such chemicals in the brain may require learning new social skills to replace those patterns of thought and behavior instilled while under the influence. For example, a long-term drug addict who stops using drugs still has to learn new social skills to replace those he learned while he was a drug addict who socialized primarily with other drug addicts.

Drug addicts and mental patients are not emotionally available while under the influence of their disorders. Their thought processes and forms of interaction, communication and emotional expression are distortions of normal thought processes. Not only are such men emotionally unavailable while in these states, they also often lack the social interaction skills that are a prerequisite for becoming emotionally available. They don't know what normal behavior is or how to engage in it. Normal adults have little interest in interacting with drug addicts, alcoholics and schizophrenics. A normal adult has nothing to gain, and may have a lot to lose, in futile or pointless social interactions with such individuals. Men under the influence of these disorders do not have fully functional minds, and the degree to which their disorders disturb their lives is also the degree to which their disorders disrupt normal emotional expression.

Drug addicts and mental patients are frozen into single roles where their problems define and limit their ability to take on, or be accepted in, other roles other than those related to their problems. They must first put their problems behind them in order to begin taking on other social roles, learn new social skills and eventually learn to become emotionally available. The problem is, that drug addicts and mental patients usually socialize primarily with their own kind, reducing their opportunities to interact with those in other roles, which operates to freeze them in their emotionally unavailable, non-adult roles. Again, they often have no idea what normal behavior is.

These syndromes effectively emit massive jamming signals that obliterate the transmission and reception of the neurotransmitter signals our brains generate to guide our thoughts and actions, leaving only warped signals and static in their wake. The way to emerge from these syndromes is to turn off the jamming signals at the source and keep them off. For drug addicts, this means ceasing the use of drugs.

For mental patients, this means taking whatever medications are available to stop their brain chemistry problems from becoming unmanageable. Jamming signals add nothing to your life and only slow you down.

Married To The Bottle

Alcohol is medically categorized as a central nervous system depressant that slows down and impairs the normal functioning of the brain and the body. Alcoholism is a common drug addiction that smoothers and distorts the higher mental functions of the human parts of the mind with lower-order addiction-influenced thought processes. Some men are married to their alcoholic role. Social reinforcement, habit and psychological/biological addiction keep them in that role. They drink and socialize primarily with other alcoholics, which reduces their opportunities to learn about, and take on, non-alcoholic social roles.

Alcoholics have divided emotional loyalties. Emotional availability is dependent on higher-order thought processes, and emotional availability fades into the background as alcohol envelops the picture. Probably the only women who can really relate to alcohol–addicted men are women who are themselves married to the bottle, and emotional availability is warped or nonexistent in any three-way relationship where one of the participants is a chemical compound.

Regardless of the details of such relationships, the fact remains that alcoholic men have deeply entrenched psychological problems that militate against not only being emotionally available but also against being in relationships and even against fulfilling an sort of non-addicted role – adult or even adolescent – due to the power of their disease.

Anything that disrupts the higher-order thought processes is almost guaranteed to disrupt emotional availability, just as random noises of sufficient volume can drown out the most enchanting of melodies. Alcoholics just have to stop drinking and learn social skills appropriate for dealing with emotionally mature non-alcoholics.

Dominance, Submission And Emotional Availability

Dominance and submission disrupt or eliminate the potential for emotional availability. Dominance is a form of communication where one person is in primary or total control of a relationship, including whatever forms of communication are allowed within the relationship.

Dominance reduces, or eliminates, the possibility of the domineering person being emotionally available because domination necessarily blocks or disrupts the possibility of two-way, self-disclosing communication, relegating the submissive partner's needs to secondary importance or even total irrelevance.

Dominance is essentially a single role that blocks true adult roles from being taken on by the dominant partner, thereby increasing or reinforcing reliance on the dominant role as that person's focus of self-definition. As dominance increases, communication and emotional expression decrease. Dominance also blocks the person under the control of the domineering partner from taking on more autonomous adult roles, thereby reducing their potential for learning new social competencies.

For example, a wife under the control of a dominant husband might be prevented from taking on a job outside the home because he does not want her to change in ways he can not predict and control. He does not want her to become independent of the role he has chosen for her, or for her to take on multiple social roles that might operate to make her more adult and independent.

Submission is also a role that reduces emotional expression and availability. Submission relegates the submissive partner's needs for emotional expression and availability to whatever status or level of importance the dominant partner assigns. Submission is a non-adult role with no room for emotional growth or expression. It necessarily blocks one from taking on other roles, at least when one is with the dominant partner.

Taking a submissive role blocks the realization of complete adult status in proportion to the degree to which the submissive role encompasses the personality and forecloses other possibilities. Someone submissive to another person's will cannot be emotionally available if they are repressing themselves from becoming a more complete adult, meaning someone who takes on varied social roles, or enter emotionally available relationships.

Adult relationships are impossible with someone who allows only top-down communication. The above definitions of dominance and submission do not apply to consensual, emotionally available adult relationships of the chains-and-leather-fetishes variety. In those situations, consenting adults engage in ritualized, agreed-upon role-playing behavior as a means of sexual excitation and role-related stimulation, rather than as a means of limiting expression altogether.

Instinctual Roles

Instinctual roles are inborn forms of behavior. They are not learned or acquired through socialization and interactions with other people. Instinctual roles are inborn, in the sense of arising out of the human genetic code. Men are genetically programmed to act in certain ways that were useful in our pre-human evolutionary past, but which we now socialize and educate men to replace with socially approved forms of substitute behavior more appropriate for our present social environment, such as substituting workplace competition for armed combat.

Purely instinctual roles leave no room for learned behavior or emotional availability, itself a form of learned behavior. Playboys, habitually violent men and habitually dominant men are common instinctual roles.

Playboys act with reproductive abandon, just as their ancestors did in a social world where a large percentage of men (and their prehuman precursors) died in intertribal warfare and while hunting animals, resulting in a social environment with many fewer unattached men than women. Men evolved over the course of millions of years in an ancestral environment where being a sort of prehistoric playboy was a common social role.

Many prehistoric women preferred the attentions of playboys to no male attention at all, given that many potential mates had died off in hunting and warfare. Playboys reproduced more often than non-playboys, and the genes of those ancestral playboys eventually permeated the human gene pool. When men fail to learn how to be emotionally available, the instinctual playboy role becomes their default social role.

Physical aggression was a useful trait in ancient times when our distant ancestors ran the risk of being killed by others over the limited supply of food, competition for mates or just generalized outbursts of frustration-based aggression. Dominance is really a form of expression of primate aggression, which allowed the most powerful primate in a group to keep all of the female breeding primates under his personal control and prevent them from breeding with other male primates. Male primates do not like to provide for offspring who do not share their genes. Dominance is thus a more primitive cousin of the playboy syndrome of instinctual behavior, and playboys are thus related to the dominant types. Both are instinctual roles.

Physical aggression is an adaptive mechanism frustrated men use when they lack of status. As frustrations over their lack of status mount, the rational human parts of the mind dissolve under stress and the instinctual animal underneath pushes through.

When the lack of status results in a lack of serotonin, physical aggression becomes more likely to erupt because frustrated men lack the serotonin-induced inner calm that status confers. This made sense back in the Stone Age world, where low-status men simply went hunting, worked out their aggressive frustrations out on a meat animal or two, brought it back to the tribe and were awarded the social status of successful hunters and the attendant psychological benefits.

Nowadays, most men channel their aggressive tendencies into culturally-approved forms of aggression, such as on the job competition or sports, but poorly-socialized men still fall back on instinctually-motivated physical aggression when their social status frustrations boil out. Violent men are not emotionally available, because purely instinctual behavior as a dominant personality characteristic precludes and overrides learned behavior such as emotional availability. Of course, every man and woman is capable of physical aggression when attacked physically, but self-defense is not what most people engage in most of their waking hours.

Emotions unmodified by some sort of learned behavior are little above animal behavior. Instinctual men exhibit underlying behavior that blindly follows the tug on the leash of their primate genes, regardless of the extent to which they mimic some outward aspects of emotionally available behavior.

Instinctual men are good at imitation, but not at adapting of their instinct-dominated one-role lives to diverse social audiences. They are no more emotionally available than a tape recorder that plays the voice of an emotionally available man is itself emotionally available. Both the machine and the instinctual man are emotionally inert.

Women claim to be attracted to men who are "secure" and "confident." What they are really saying is that they are attracted to men who appear secure because they have taken on multiple social roles, and derive various forms of psychological calm from having taken on those roles. Inner security is a result of serotonin in the body, and having serotonin in the body is a result of the mind's perception of the recognition of social status by other people.

They feel confident about themselves precisely because they have a track record of successful adaptation to coping with the challenges that diverse social environments require and have an objective basis for feeling confident. They know that they can cope with life's stresses and situations, and see no reason to walk around with their tail between their legs. They are not worried about letting go emotionally, because they have reserves of inner security to spare.

Insecure men lack confidence because the limited role or roles they take on provide few opportunities to become more complete adults by adapting themselves to diverse social contexts. These men know they lack the status to compete with other men, so they back off from open competition and set up their own value systems. A street gang that says nine-to-five jobs are bad according to the gang's standards of value. Being "cool" and disinterested in work is their social norm. The rest of the world, including women, goes about its business as usual, not caring what such men agree upon among themselves. They offer nothing that the rest of the world cares about. When insecure men set up such contrary value systems, they simply reinforce their preexisting psychological problems and plough themselves deeper under than before.

How Dependency Blocks Emotional Availability

Dependency is an all-encompassing non-adult role that spills over into many areas of life, smothering a man's potential for emotional availability and even his capacity for self-support. Dependency is a single role, usually learned early in life, that operates to block off opportunities to learn how to take on other roles and become emotionally available.

One common form is an adult man who lives with his mother or father. He takes on a dependent-son role that precludes him from opportunities to take on other roles that might expand his opportunities for independence, such as when he feels he needs to consult his mother about bringing a lady friend home for the weekend.

Dependent men tend to shy away from disclosing themselves to others, because disclosing what a mess they've made of their lives gets them nowhere. Neurotic concern about what his mother might think about his plans is a sure-fire extinguisher of spontaneity and other distinguishing characteristics of emotional availability. The more practice a man gets at being dependent on relatives, the more ingrained that role becomes and the more it permeates other parts of his life.

True adults have nothing to gain from interactions with dependent non-adults. Adults find it tiresome to have protracted contact with someone who refers to his mother in every second sentence and says he has to "check" with his mother about staying out late. Such habits of dependency are to be expected of adolescents, but are grotesque in chronological adults with normal mental faculties.

Autonomy and independence are adult capacities and prerequisites for becoming emotionally available. Locking yourself into a dependent role means choosing to freeze yourself into an adolescent role. It becomes increasingly difficult to escape from this role over time. A dependent man misses out on more and more opportunities with each passing year to mature, and looks less and less desirable to others as a potential companion as time goes on. Emotionally mature adults have better things to do with their time.

Dependency can also be linked to other self-limiting roles, such as alcoholism. Linking two or more dependent roles effectively bars the individual from being considered an emotionally available adult by emotionally available women. Only women with similar problems see kindred souls in such men. Having problems in common does not mean they have much of anything else in common, however. Two such people have little to offer each other beyond companionship in misery, rather than the potential for stimulating adult relationships. They can only offer each other what they bring to the table with them.

Homosexual Roles

Homosexuals act out roles for public and private audiences of one or more men. Homosexual roles and lifestyles necessarily exclude performing for private female audiences and militate against developing emotional availability with women. Homosexuals get no practice at developing heterosexual intimacy and emotional availability, and consequently do not develop it. Women typically assume, at best, some sort of non-sexual "buddy" role in the social universe of homosexual males.

Changing a confirmed homosexual is a difficult task. It goes against the grain of decades of voluntarily chosen lifestyle choices and sexual experiences on the part of homosexuals. The homosexual mentality of being open only with other men can become deeply embedded in a man's personality to the extent that they see no reason to change, and no benefit from learning to identify with women and deal with women as potential romantic companions, given the ground rules they choose to live by. Acting out a homosexual role is a variation of the role men take on in other male-on-male peer groups.

They take on roles and cater to the role expectations of those within the homosexual peer group. Thus, while heterosexual men seek out women, homosexuals are largely self-made prisoners of their roles. They do not seek out women due to a combination of social conditioning and choices they freely made, and resent attempts by outsiders such as women to force change upon them. Like other one-role men, the more time they spend in their single roles, the more natural those single roles seem to them, though not to others.

Rigidly Scripted Roles

The greater the extent to which a man lives out some rigidly scripted, ritualized role as his primary social role, the more increasingly likely it is that the man is an emotionally hollow shell. Why? Rigidly scripted roles are the opposite of the self-disclosing spontaneity that is a prerequisite for emotional availability. Rigidly scripted roles are designed to impress external social audiences, such as male peer groups, with how well a man meets their expectations. They have nothing to do with emotional self-expression.

A man might be obsessed with living a role round the clock, deliberately leaving himself no time to think about what he prefers to be when not on a public stage acting out a role. The more rigidly scripted the conformist role, less room left for spontaneity and individuality. The greater the degree to which one role scripts a man's entire life, the greater the degree to which that role defines emotional availability as irrelevant to that role.

One common rigidly scripted role is the man who strives to always dress and look his best. Women infer qualities about men based on appearance, and dress plays a major part in shaping female perceptions. A man consumed by the desire to always look his best is acting out some sort of role in an attempt to manipulate how women perceive him.

The usual aim of such men is to manipulate their female audiences towards covert sexual or financial goals he maps out. The more a man preens in front of a mirror, the more suspicious and ready to move on a woman should be. Male attire is a stage prop or costume for the roles men take on. You can't trust a man who acts out a role round the clock. Where is his individuality and spontaneity? Men obsessed with their personal fronts are not emotionally available, because emotional availability requires relaxed spontaneity, something constantly-tended personal fronts automatically exclude. Emotional availability emerges when you drop your public roles to take on a private role for a companion in intimacy, not what you use to manipulate others.

Such men use impression management to make their private female audiences sing the tones the manipulator wants to hear, like a violinist playing his violin just so with his bow to make the music he knows touching the violin just so will elicit. There's no reason for a man to always be preening, unless there's nothing behind his mask, or something he does not want you to see. Men obsessed with external appearance have no time for the hidden world of emotions.

Playing a rigidly scripted role that mimics the appearance of emotional availability is an inert substitute for emotional availability used by emotionally unavailable men. If every move he makes seems rehearsed, what you see of him is a carefully-scripted act. If you ask him an unexpected question and you get either a blank look or a prerecorded message, he is pulling the wool over your eyes. Such men pretend to be emotionally available or romantic to get what they want from women, who expect at least lip service to the idea of emotional availability. The more limited the man's capacities for emotional availability, the less multidimensional his personality and the more he falls back on phony, second-hand scripted roles copied from others, as opposed to expressing the hidden emotions of his undesirable true self.

Women often mistakenly confuse the role being played with the man playing the role. A man is not emotionally available just because he takes on a certain role. A role is no more the man behind the role than a movie projected on a screen is a physical reality. Women should not confuse the role with the man performing the symbolization represented by the role, meaning the underlying core personality of the man and what he really is.

Don't read anything into the blanks. Just because a man fills a role to perfection, such as being a doctor, does not mean anything else about him is perfect or wonderful. He might be great in fulfilling that one role, and a total washout in other parts of life outside that role. Don't think some other qualities you do not observe are actually there until you see some evidence of them.

The Shadow Of Fraud

Some men will not work to develop core personalities or take on multiple roles. They pick a single role to carry themselves through life: fraud. A fraud makes a career out of deceiving others and pretending to be what he is not to obtain benefits from others by creating false impressions of themselves in others. As regards personal relationships, the most common type of fraud is the type of man who uses a variety of stereotypical phrases, sophisticated manners and expert taste in clothing, all of which are tailored to impress women as a means of obtaining sexual favors and money from women. Such men are shadows without substance. They have put on such smoke-and-mirrors acts precisely because they offer women nothing of substance. Fraud tends to be a way of life for such men, because they are unwilling to put out the effort that taking on other roles requires. Frauds are one-role men in every part of their lives. Whether by intent or default, there is less to them than meets the eye. Such men are living lies.

Frauds can't cut it in life, so they have no choice but to use various forms of deception to promote their self-interests. They can not get through life any other way. Taking on other roles is not an option for frauds, because the underlying premise of being a fraud – deception – precludes them from considering taking on other roles or becoming emotionally available. There's no opportunity for deception in leading an honest life and honestly filling out multiple social roles and edging into greater degrees of self-disclosure. Remember that being emotionally available requires self-disclosure, the last thing in the world a fraud intends to practice. A man doesn't have any feelings for a woman worth talking about if he is intent on completely deceiving her.

Men who lack what normal men pick up in the course of taking on social roles, such as a work ethic, have to be extremely good at taking on inauthentic roles and generating misleading impressions in the minds of others or they will fall by the wayside in short order. No woman who faces the facts would ever want to have contact with a fraud, so such men must work very hard at convincing women that they are something other than what they really are by means of acting out rigidly scripted roles and projecting reassuring personal fronts.

If you can predict almost everything about a man and what he will say, he is probably a fraud. If he is a perfect dresser and dancer, you may have a lot to worry about. Most men couldn't care less about how they dress unless forced to by the roles they take on (such as a job), and dancing is not a skill incorporated into the male genetic code. The more perfect he seems, the more likely he is to be a wholly false construct designed with one thing in mind – to get women to do what he wants by setting them at their ease and turning off the alarms that should go off in the head.

The more a man talks like something out of a romance novel or movie, sources from which frauds know naïve women get their ideas about men, the more certain you can be that his lines really are lifted from romance novels and movies. Most frauds mix financial business and sexual pleasure. They manipulate one woman after another, going through the life's savings of one woman after another before skipping town, leaving only memories of the shadows they cast over the lives of the women they knew.

Normal men have idiosyncrasies and hidden corners of the personality that surprise even their wives after decades of marriage. Nobody is so limited in scope that you can know everything about them, and every normal man has a few things that don't quite fit with the rest of their personality. For example, an otherwise predictably sedate accountant might have discordant or even bizarre secret hobbies, such as watching mud wrestling or collecting knots of barbed wire. If you can predict everything about a man, chances are he is putting on some sort of act or hiding something. When every part of a man seems to click together perfectly into a smoothly coherent whole, he is almost always hiding something. Normal men always have some unusual quirks or bizarre habits or hobbies you will find out about once you get to know them.

Emotionally available men are spontaneous and have autonomous tendencies. Spontaneity means doing unpredictable things now and then, in both intimate and non-intimate situations. The two correlate inversely: the more emotionally available a man is, the more spontaneous he is in most parts of his life. The less emotionally available he is, the more predictable and unspontaneous he is in everything he says and does, and the more likely it is that he is a fraud. The more one social role dominates his life, the more you can predict about him. If he never gets you upset and is always calmly reassuring, be on your watch. The spontaneity that accompanies emotional availability should present you with a man with a variety of little quirks and anomalies.

Women can also be frauds. Women who stage faked accidents to get control of a relationship or just to feel important are frauds. They have no other way to feel they are in control. Women who fraudulently cast themselves in victim roles to control men are frauds. Women's prisons are filled with female frauds and other types of female criminals.

Frauds And Liars

Frauds deceive women about their true personalities and lives because deceiving women leads to what they consider positive sexual and financial experiences. Such men have no alternative way of obtaining such positive experiences, given the role-taking limitations they choose to impose on themselves. To the uninformed observer, frauds might seem to be taking on multiple social roles, but that is not actually

189

the case. Conning women is just one aspect of an underlying single-role personality they exhibit in other social contexts as well.

Frauds differ from liars. Liars tend to engage in spur-of-the-moment deceptive behavior, whereas frauds tend to plan every aspect of what they say and do in advance, including their appearances. Liars tell whatever opportunistic lies come to mind, usually in the context of a sexual encounter, to get the woman to open up sexually. Some men will eat whatever they see first if they are hungry, and sexually hungry liars will say whatever comes to mind that will facilitate their access to sex. Liars are essentially opportunists who use lies to take advantage of whatever opportunities the situation of the moment offers. Liars are usually found telling endless lies in other social contexts whenever they can get away with it, but typically fulfill some sort of semi-productive social role in order to get themselves through life. That role might be nothing better than a conformist, if self-supporting, member of some sort of male group.

Frauds are parasites who can not cut it in life without victims to manipulate into making up the deficits that frauds pile up. A fraud without victims will not go very far in life. Every role the fraud seems to fulfill is actually centers around fraud, deceiving of others to obtain benefits frauds are unable or unwilling to earn by their own efforts. Frauds are incapable of real relationships, because long term exposure to their victims might lead to them being recognized for what they are and experiencing legal or physical retaliation. Any role a fraud seems to fulfill is simply a manifestation of the single role of fraud, their core role and personality trait.

Frauds are quite practiced at stringing along victims with endless promises, the only thing frauds can offer. Any contact a fraud initiates is carefully crafted to get prospective victims to let down their offenses and let the fraud browse around for ways to take advantage of the situation.

The more polished a man's personal front, manner and attire, the more perfect he seem to be, the more plausible the excuses he calmly offers – those are the trademarks of a fraud. If he never raises his voice, he's a fraud. If he always talks in a calm, unemotional, silky-smooth monotone, he's a fraud. He's just an actor on a stage using women as his audience or stage props. His seeming perfection is only a form of expression of the polish with which he plays his role.

Check out the facts of whatever he says, and you'll soon find it to be either completely unverifiable or a lie from beginning to end. The only way to deal with a fraud is to have no dealings whatsoever with them. Frauds will no more change their ways than wolves will change their ways, and are as emotionally available as wolves.

Chapter Nine
Meeting Emotionally
Available Men

Sorting Out Emotionally
Available And Unavailable Men

Emotionally available men usually seek emotionally available women, should they not already be so involved. Yes, some of the good ones, though hardly all, are already taken. The problem with separating the wheat from the chaff is that emotionally available men don't wear T-shirts with brand names advertising their personal qualities.

The opposite is sometimes true, however: emotionally unavailable men sometimes do unwittingly advertise their emotional unavailability. A man wearing a gang jacket, for example, is almost certainly emotionally unavailable. The gang jacket advertises how he defines himself. The bond he shares with his fellow gang members is a large part of what defines him. He considers this group-identification bond so central to his self-definition that he feels he must wear his group membership on his sleeve, so to speak.

The minds of such men are so overloaded with male peer group bonds that little room remains for anything involving women except out on the periphery of emotional relevance.

It is not worth your bother to try and sort out the rare exceptions to this principle. So many men offer something better than emotional unavailability that there is no good reason to waste your time on low-probability prospects wearing gang jackets advertising that they think their peer group memberships define them. Fraternities are just the middle-class version of street gangs, and the greater the degree to which a fraternity member, both in school and after graduation, defines himself in terms of male peer-group affiliations is the degree to which he is unsuitable for adult relationships, regardless of social class.

The same principle applies to viciously bizarre or defamatory tattoos. These are actually more permanent versions of gang jackets worn under the skin instead of on top of it, whether those wearing them are in gangs or not. Men sporting nasty tattoos or bizarre images etched onto their bodies are actually broadcasting what is on their minds. Such tattoos are actually examples of self-mutilation reflecting underlying poor self-images, traits not usually associated with emotional availability. Men with poor self-images sporting such Rorschach-style body art advertise how few pluses they can bring to relationships. Branding peer group affiliations and off-the-wall personal statements onto one's body is more of the same. Their group membership notions and mental problems are more important to them than the esthetics of their bodies.

Most women want little do with men who have delusions and borderline psychoses floating around upstairs. When a man has a tattoo artist embed an image or words into his body, what he is really doing is attempting to freeze his self-image into whatever random thoughts he fancies at the moment, forgetting that getting through life will involve continual adjustments to various social contexts throughout life. The tattoo or brand he gets as an adolescent to prove his dedication to the local gang will look like a bad joke on the beach ten years later, and few newlywed women would think of rubbing their husband's gang brand for good luck.

There are a few other major ways to screen out the obvious, and somewhat less obvious, nonstarter types. Men who won't work and won't look for work are always bad news. Their entire self-definition revolves on remaining unemployed and unemployable. They choose to freeze themselves into a single role that prevents them from taking on other social roles such as that of self-supporting adult.

Avoid certain types of men, particularly peer groups of men of any age, whose social activities revolve around alcohol, unemployment, nonstop athletics activities, rowdy spectator sports, anti-intellectualism or thinly disguised envy of those better off than themselves. Regardless of the reasons they give for being so, men with such tendencies are bad bets for emotional availability. Their mindsets are contrary to the spontaneous, communicative, truthful, emotionally available mindset. Emotional availability requires a man with a fully functioning mind, not someone who can't be bothered to make the effort to turn his mind on in the first place. Remember that emotional availability is a learned or acquired trait men develop as a byproduct of emotional socialization. It is not an inborn instinct, but rather a skill that men slowly learn to develop by adapting their behavior to being with women. Men with no interest in learning new tricks probably don't want to learn how one woman differs from another woman either.

Men can change. In the case of men who persist in acting in an immature manner due to peer-group influences, they simply have to separate themselves from those groups and think for themselves. This might require moving far enough away from the groups that are the cause of the problem for them to no longer be an influence. Moving to another city to accept a job is a good idea in such cases. Moving out of one's parents home is another good idea. Anything that encourages a man to take on different adult social roles is generally a good thing for men who have little or no experience being real adults who can routinely take on multiple social roles.

Talking Means Two-Way Communication

Meeting emotionally available men requires talking with them at length. You must talk with a man for an extended period of time to get to know him well enough to discover whether or not he is emotionally available. Emotional availability is a form of communication, and there is no way you can determine emotional availability without doing some communicating of your own. If you think you can just stand on the sidelines and find out by telepathy, by taking a fast glance or by asking one of your girlfriends, you are completely wrong. You can no more understand a man at first glance than you can tell a book by its cover. You have to look through his table of contents, and that requires taking the time to talk with him long enough to browse his table of contents. Women who can't be bothered to talk long enough to find out what a man is like will find themselves settling for pigs in a poke of uncertain emotional character.

You will not like every man you talk with, and you will most likely have to sift through a large field of men to find someone both emotionally available and personally compatible. There is no substitute for talking with the men yourself. No amount of talking it over with your girlfriends or mother, or wishing for the right man to drop into your lap with no effort on your part, will make him materialize. Regardless of how you meet a man, you absolutely must talk with him if you want to get a relationship going. If you do not talk with men, you'll never meet men in the first place, let alone find an emotionally available one. Not talking means not having a relationship.

It's hard to uncover much of anything about a man when you fail to make initial casual social contact with him. You don't know enough about him to respond to him in a way that shows that you are interested enough in him to adjust to being with him. Just taking a fast look tells you almost nothing about him except what he chooses to wear and whether he got a good night's sleep. Prolonged conversational contact can tell you a lot more, however, and you can try to initiate prolonged contact on your own.

Should you appear to be tuned into acting out a role for some other social audience, such as your girlfriends or mother, men will simply not bother to communicate with you. The role they see you playing for women offers nothing to a male social audience, however much it offers to other women. Remember, you must fine-tune your behavior to show that you are interested in what men in general have to offer, as well as what one particular man might offer.

Playing hard to get means you will meet men who see hard-to-get women as habitual leisure time pursuits who come to them unburdened with long-term emotional consequences. Should a woman fail to disclose anything about what she is really like, she gives a man nothing to be interested in beyond the purely physical, because all he knows about her is that she is a woman who exhibits stereotyped, nonindividualistic behavior. The less of an individual you seem to be, the more men will treat you as a generic, undifferentiated member of the female category, because you give them no reason to treat you as an individual.

Many women feel inhibited about trying to pick up men, meaning attempting to initiate conversations with men with whom they have no prior relationship. This is simply a bad habit women fall into as a byproduct of the social roles they take on and practice. The expectation of the audience, usually meaning some group of unattached women, is that "nice" women should not do things like that. The reality is that it comes down to something other women expect you to do to meet their need to see you conform to their lowest-common-denominator expectations that you not make them envious of your social success. This meets their needs, not yours.

Remember, allowing your public social roles and associated habits of mind to influence your private life is a guaranteed disaster. You will have nothing to show for your efforts to do what other women expect of you. Keep in mind that women must sometimes take the initiative, as when you see someone you sense might have potential walking by and he is not in a position to see you. Opportunities that pass you by will probably never come your way again. Don't let this happen to you.

Men don't know what you are thinking, but they do know what they see and hear, and what they see and hear of you is what they think you are really like. If you don't look emotionally available, they will assume that you are not. Conversely, appearing to be emotionally available is thus only a notch below actually being emotionally available. You can do certain things that spell out to men that you are likely to be emotionally available. You can express your emotional availability both verbally and nonverbally using eye contact, smiling, gestures, facial expressions and tone of voice to communicate what sort of woman you are. Should you not want to communicate or otherwise express some indications of your emotional availability potential, you will wind up with emotionally unavailable men. Rightly or wrongly, men will assume that what they see and hear of you is all there is to you. If there is more, it is up to you to go out of your way to publicly broadcast what you are really like. Emotionally available men do not care for emotional adolescents, or for women who give the appearance of being emotionally unavailable. Talking does not mean grilling or interviewing him as if you are checking off characteristics on a list.

Making initial contact with an emotionally available man is a two-way experience. This means that, should he have an interest in you, he will do much the same in communicating as you should be doing. In addition to talking with you, he will also make direct eye contact with you, smile, show a range of facial expression and maybe make a few gestures. If you can't do the same, he will have no alternative but to assume that you have little interest in him. Remember, men can not see what goes on in your head. What you allow them to see and hear of you is what they will assume you are really like. From the point of view of the man, the woman who does not show herself to be emotionally available is not emotionally available, as far as men are concerned. You need to express an obvious interest in him or else he will assume that you don't care, given the absence of evidence to the contrary.

Listening To Emotionally Available Men

Emotionally unavailable men talk in different ways, and about different things, than do emotionally available men. Should a man say negative things about women in general, he is probably bad news. His emotional unavailability has pushed him into a corner where the only women he meets are similarly emotionally unavailable women, resulting in him having nothing good to say about women. He winds up meeting only women with negative personalities just like his own, and other types of women avoid him. He offers them nothing that interests them.

Should a man's conversation keep drifting back to what others think of him or how they react to him, particularly a group of male colleagues such co-workers or relatives, he is bad news. Emotionally available men have core personalities independent of the audiences for whom they take on roles. An ongoing preoccupation with what some group thinks of him means he lacks the individuality to develop an individualistic personality suitable for emotional involvement. The emotionally unavailable man's primary frame of reference is what other groups of people think, not what he thinks of himself or adjusting to being with one particular woman. If he can't tune out some out-of-sight male social audience and tune in his female social audience in the here-and-now, forget him.

Several examples can help illustrate this. If all a man can talk about is what his male peer group of overaged drinking cohorts thinks of him, forget him. The greater his focus on playing a role for a group of men with whom he shares a common bond, the less emotional energy he has left for you. If all a man over the age of twenty-one can talk about is sports, which are actually ritualized forms of aggression or combat, there's nothing in such experiences and activities on which you can base a relationship. Bonds based on ritualized combat or adolescent male social group bonds have no carryover value that will bear emotional fruit if applied to adult male-female relationships. Men whose lives and manner of speech show no signs of efforts to identify with women, and no corresponding signs of efforts to adjust their thinking and behavior to being with women, offer women nothing on which to ground relationships.

What other sorts of positive things should a woman look for in emotionally available men? The first is some evidence of compassion or empathy, both of which reflect an underlying ability to identify with women, in the sense that they can put themselves in a woman's shoes, and get some idea about how a woman wants to be treated. Anything else is just play-acting. A man who can't identify with women will never be emotionally available, because he can not understand what the other person feels and thinks. He offers nothing on which you can base two-way emotional communications. A man who can't identify with others can't take on roles tailored to a woman's needs and expectations and will fail to develop the adult communications skills he needs for intimate, one-on-one communications. He neither understands a woman's needs nor can he adapt his own thoughts and behavior when he is with women.

The ability to identify with a woman is thus the key trait a woman should look for in a man. The second trait is whether or not he can take on multiple adult social roles. If he can't identify with others and see things from their angle, he can't take on roles that meet the expectations and needs of women. He doesn't know what they expect of him and probably doesn't care what others think of him either. Men unable to identify with others can't take on multiple roles, can't adjust to dealing with different types of people and can't effectively communicate with them. They remain frozen in some variant of a self-centered, egocentric role that reflects their continuing inability to understand others and adjust their speech, thoughts and behavior to women.

Strong silent types are bad news. Emotionally available men are communicative, and disclose what they are like because they like themselves just the way they are. Strong silent types have nothing to say because they have nothing going on upstairs, intellectually or emotionally speaking. If they have something to say or disclose, why don't they say it? The most likely reason is that they have worked at fined-tuning themselves for emotionally distant, uncommunicative relationships, meaning superficial and purely sexual relationships. Remaining silent lets naive women project anything onto such men whatever they wish was true, while the reality is that there's almost nothing going on upstairs. If a grown man won't tell you what he thinks of you and how he feels about you, you probably have a lot to worry about, and definitely nothing on which to base a relationship.

Emotionally available men have a sense of humor. They can stand outside their social roles and laugh at themselves and others. A man who can't laugh at himself takes himself and his social role or roles too seriously. He is socially rigid to the extent of locking himself into a single social role that renders him unable to see himself as others see him. He can't identify with others and thus cannot see himself from an outsider's perspective. Emotionally unavailable men don't have much of a sense of humor. They take themselves and their limited social roles and social arenas too seriously. They are neither emotionally nor socially experienced enough to develop a real sense of humor.

Emotionally available men have some sort of intellectual interests, though they are not necessarily bookish. Intellectual interests here means knowledge of an acquired nature, rather than purely instinctual, self-centered matters such as their sexual appetites, how aggressive they are and how important they think they are because they take on some single social role. Such topics of discussion are examples of purely instinctual behavior at the opposite end of the spectrum from the strictly intellectual, which requires the acquisition of information or knowledge from external sources, to say nothing of learning to control or moderate one's instinctual passions. If he has nothing to talk about beyond his personal activities and sense of self-importance, there is probably nothing more to him than meets the eye.

Emotionally available men disclose what they are really like without a lot of bluster or attempts to conceal their true nature. The most important thing to keep in kind is that, whatever the details, they do have a core personality underneath. There's more to them than meets the eye at first glance. If a man can't, or won't, tell you anything about how he reacts and relates to different kinds of people, and what he learned about himself from dealing with them, his personality may be null and void as far as you are concerned. Emotionally available men are confident about being accepted for what they are, so they are not afraid of self-disclosure. This does not necessarily mean, however, that they will disclose everything about themselves to the first casual stranger who happens to ask.

Individuality is the home base of the heart, because emotions are highly individualized concerns that derive from the individual's reactions to people and circumstances. The individual expresses his very personal emotional reactions to his personal estimation of how people and circumstances impact him and his loved ones. Without individuality, there are no real emotions, just emotions derived from imitating others and living up others' expectation about how he should think and act.

If a man's manner of speech is peppered with endless references to what others think of him, he is no more an individual capable of individual emotional expression and bonding than a mass-produced plaster statue that mimics a man's form but is just inert material inside.

Emotionally available men are spontaneous, meaning they are known to say and do things on the spur of the moment and off the top of their heads, at least on occasion. Unspontaneous men are rigid conformists incapable of being emotionally available because controlling their spontaneity means controlling other parts of the personality related to emotions as well. If everything a man says sounds like he read them somewhere, heard them from others or just seems calculated to not offend anyone, he is a bad bet for a relationship. Such men want everything planned ahead of time.

The presence or absence of exclusionary bonds with other men can be determined by talking with a man and noting whether he adjusts his manner of speech to being with a woman. Should a man talk with you the same way he talks with men, forget him. His ingrained male-buddy role has conditioned him to think, talk and act in certain ways, including his manner of speech, setting limits on emotional expression with women.

Only men whose minds are not filled to the brim with exclusionary male peer group bonds that preclude emotional bonds with women have the potential to become good bets for relationships. If his apparent frame of reference or mindset is how he fits in with a group of drinking partners, forget him.

If all of a man's speech and behavior seem to derive from unconsciously acting out a single social role, he is emotionally unavailable and can never adjust his behavior to meet your emotional needs. The other role or roles determine the emotional and behavioral limitations of what he is open to doing and expressing with you. His inability to adjust his speech to being with a woman reflects an underlying inability to adjust his thoughts, behavior and understanding to meeting a woman's needs. You do not need to get involved with a man who puts a higher priority on what third parties think of how he acts than the value he puts on what you think of him. Men who can't tune out other social roles when in an informal context with women are best forgotten as soon as possible.

No Man is Always Emotionally Available

Emotionally available men can feel just as stressed as anyone else in particularly stressful circumstances or life situations. For example, should they lose their jobs, they will be understandably nervous about paying their food and rent bills. Emotionally available men do not see it as the end of their world, however. It's just a problem be worked through. They might be stressed out, however, and, depending on the details of their circumstances, be under so much short-term stress that whatever you try to say will just not really get through to them. Stress blocks emotional availability.

Try to help a guy with potential get out of his pickle should you have anything relevant to impart, and jot down his name and phone number for future reference. Future reference means after things start going well for him again. Don't press issues like getting involved and long term commitments with a man who is still in the process of bottoming out or who feels as if he is on the edge of a psychological cliff. Give him some time to climb a few notches up the curve. The same applies to emotionally available men already involved with someone else. Wait until they reenter the singles market, but don't count on that happening in a way that suits your personal timetable or agenda. In the meantime, see if he can introduce you to some of his single male friends, who are probably a few notches more likely than average to be emotionally available themselves. Emotionally available men tend to associate with both women and other men with similar frames of reference.

The Men Behind The Roles

A woman who sees a man taking on a certain role might see that one small, scripted and possibly inauthentic part of a man's life and make a snap judgment about him and his life as whole, including emotional availability. This is a mistake. A role is not the man, and a man is − or should be − more than the sum of the role he takes on for others. Just because you see a man playing a role, such as being a hard worker, does not mean he either takes on other roles has a core personality autonomous of his roles, or even fills out his role well over the long run. The smaller the segment of his total behavior you see, the less reliably you can generalize it to sum him up as a total person. You need more information, and talking with him is the way to get most of it.

Just as you can't assume that a man is anything like a rock star just because he dresses like one, don't assume that he's just like your emotionally available, happily-married Uncle John because he dresses like him, talks like him or has the same job as Uncle John. He might just be an actor, all show and nothing behind the facade. You might observe a man filling out one particular role he might not take to heart, such as a job he hates. Don't over-generalize and fill in the blanks about a man's personality with wishful thinking about the many other parts of his life, including emotional availability, regardless of whether what you see of him reminds you of someone else who takes on a similar role. Wishful thinking says more about what's going on in your head than what's going on in his head.

Emotionally Available Couples

People naturally gravitate towards those like themselves in temperament and personality. It's hard to see one half of a couple being calm, confident, secure and open to what others have to offer as being paired off with an edgy, nervous, potentially violent, insecure individual who lacks confidence, poise, security and inner calm. Yet many people do just that, particularly women who think that "change" a man who has had decades of experience at becoming what he is now. Two such people are both on different wavelengths. They hail from mutually exclusive social universes where people think and live in very different ways. They have nothing in common. It is not a question of whether the relationship will break up, but rather a question of how soon it will break up. The emotionally unavailable half of the couple will bristle about their real and imagined deficiencies while wearing down the emotionally available half of the couple with a variety of put-downs and demands until they revert to spinning along on separate social orbits.

Emotionally available people speak each other's language and have the capacity to understand and enjoy being together in a spirit of mutual enjoyment and a state of facile enjoyment and communication of their needs with each other. They can step outside the role behavior that other social audiences expect of them elsewhere, tune into being with each other and make and break their own rules as they go along. Being emotionally available means adapting to being with each other, not the needs and expectations of third parties outside their private relationship. Two emotionally available people have much to offer each other, and even more to talk about when they come together as a couple.

References

Jerome H. Barkow, Leda Cosmides and John Tooby, Editors *The Adapted Mind: Evolutionary Psychology And The Generation Of Culture* Oxford University Press, 1992.

Jack Block "Ego-Identity, Role Variability, And Adjustment" *Journal Of Consulting Psychology* 1961, Volume 25, Number 3, pages 392-397.

Eileen M. Donahue, Richard W. Robins, Brent W. Roberts, and Oliver P. John "The Divided Self: Concurrent And Longitudinal Effects Of Psychological Adjustment And Social Roles On Self-Concept Differentiation" *Journal Of Personality And Social Psychology* 1993, Volume 64, Number 6, pages 834-846.

Sigmund Freud *Group Psychology And The Analysis Of The Ego* W.W. Norton and Company, 1975.

Erving Goffman *The Presentation Of Self In Everyday Life* Doubleday and Company, 1959.

Erving Goffman *Stigma: Notes On The Management Of Spoiled Identity* Prentice-Hall, 1963.

William J. Goode "A Theory Of Role Strain" *American Sociological Review* August, 1960, Volume 25, Number 4, pages 483-496.

Paul Goodman *Growing Up Absurd: Problems Of Youth In The Organized System* Random House, 1960.

Karen Horney *Our Inner Conflicts: A Constructive Theory Of Neurosis* W.W. Norton and Company, 1945.

Waynne B. James, James E. Witte and Michael W. Galbraith "Havighurst's Social Roles Revisited" *Journal Of Adult Development* March, 2006, Volume 13, Number 1, pages 52-60.

Sidney M. Jourard *The Transparent Self* Van Nostrand Reinhold, 1971.

YoungMee Kim "Cognitive Concepts Of The Self And Romantic Relationships" *Basic And Applied Social Psychology* June, 2006, Volume 28, Number 2, pages 169-175.

Gustave Le Bon *The Crowd: A Study Of The Popular Mind* Viking Press, 1960.

Patricia W. Linville "Self-Complexity And Affective Extremity: Don't Put All Of Your Eggs In One Cognitive Basket" *Social Cognition* Spring, 1985, pages 94-120.

Stephen R. Marks "Multiple Roles And Role Strain: Some Notes On Human Energy, Time And Commitment" *American Sociological Review* December, 1977, Volume 42, Number 6, pages 921-936.

Hazel Markus "Self-Schemata And Processing Information About Self" *Journal Of Personality And Social Psychology* 1977, Volume 35, Number 2, pages 63-78.

William McDougall *The Group Mind* Arno Press, 1973.

George Herbert Mead *Mind, Self & Society* University Of Chicago Press, 1934.

Thomas Mussweiler, Shira Gabriel and Galen V. Bodenhausen "Shifting Social Identities As A Strategy For Deflecting Threatening Social Comparisons" *Journal Of Personality And Social Psychology* 2000, Volume 79, Number 3, pages 398-409.

Mikael Nordenmark "Multiple Social Roles And Well-Being: A Longitudinal Test Of The Role Stress Theory And The Role Expansion Theory" *Acta Sociologica* 2004, Volume 47, Number 2, pages 115-126.

Robert Ezra Park *Race And Culture* Free Press, 1950.

David Riesman *The Lonely Crowd: A Study Of The Changing American Character* Yale University Press, 1950.

Sonia Roccas and Marilynn B. Brewer "Social Identity Complexity" *Personality And Social Psychology Review* 2002, Volume 6, Number 2, pages 88-106.

Lee Strasberg *A Dream of Passion: The Development Of The Method* Little, Brown and Company, 1987.

Frederick Milton *Thrasher The Gang: A Study Of 1,313 Gangs In Chicago* University of Chicago Press, 1963.

George Vaillant *Adaptation To Life* Little, Brown and Company, 1977.

William Hollingsworth Whyte *The Organization Man* Doubleday and Company, 1957.

Robert Wright *The Moral Animal: The New Science Of Evolutionary Psychology* Pantheon Press, 1994.

17419077R00117

Made in the USA
Lexington, KY
08 September 2012